How to Be Perfect

How to Be Perfect

One Church's
Audacious Experiment in
Living the Old Testament
Book of Leviticus

Daniel M. Harrell

New York   Boston   Nashville

Unless otherwise noted, Scripture quotations are taken from the HOLY BIBLE: NEW INTERNATIONAL VERSION® © 1973, 1978, 1984 by International Bible Society. Used by permission of Zondervan Publishing House. All rights reserved.

Other Scripture quotations are from the following sources: The English Standard Version (ESV). © 2001 by Crossway Bibles, a division of Good News Publishers. *Holy Bible*, New Living Translation (NLT) © 1996, 2004. Used by permission of Tyndale House Publishers, Inc., Wheaton, Illinois 60189. All rights reserved. NEW REVISED STANDARD VERSION of the Bible (NRSV) © 1989 by the Division of Christian Education of the National Council of the Churches of Christ in the U.S.A. All rights reserved. Today's English Version (TEV) © American Bible Society 1966, 1971, 1976, 1992. HOLY BIBLE, TODAY'S NEW INTERNATIONAL VERSION® (TNIV®) © 2001, 2005 by International Bible Society. Used by permission of Zondervan. All rights reserved. REVISED STANDARD VERSION of the Bible (RSV) © 1946, 1952, 1971, 1973 by the Division of Christian Education of the National Council of the Churches of Christ in the U.S.A. Used by permission. The King James Version (KJV). Public domain. The NEW AMERICAN STANDARD BIBLE® (NASB) © 1960, 1962, 1963, 1968, 1971, 1972, 1973, 1975, 1977, 1995 by The Lockman Foundation. Used by permission.

FaithWords
Hachette Book Group
237 Park Avenue
New York, NY 10017
www.faithwords.com

Printed in the United States of America

First Edition: January 2011

10   9   8   7   6   5   4   3   2   1

FaithWords is a division of Hachette Book Group, Inc.

The FaithWords name and logo are trademarks of Hachette Book Group, Inc.

Library of Congress Cataloging-in-Publication Data

Harrell, Daniel M.
 How to be perfect: one church's audacious experiment in living the Old Testament book of Leviticus / Daniel M. Harrell. —1st ed.
  p. cm.
Summary: "The life-changing lessons learned by church members when they tried to live out the complicated and sometimes odd laws in the Old Testament book of Leviticus for 30 days" —Provided by the publisher.
 Includes bibliographical references.
 ISBN 978-0-446-55717-7
1. Bible. O.T. Leviticus—Criticism, interpretation, etc. 2. Holiness—Biblical teaching. 3. Jewish law. 4. Park Street Church (Boston, Mass.) I. Title.

  BS1255.6.H6H37 2011
  222'.1306—dc22
              2010018976

For Violet

Contents

Contents

Acknowledgments

This project would have never been possible without the eager participation of the nineteen members of Park Street Church, Boston, who were willing to jump into the Levitical world, fully experience it, and honestly chronicle their thoughts. Brian Bassett, Brandy Brooks, Simon Chang, Christine Cos, Ophera Davis, Kim Engle, Kristen Filipic, Ian Frazier, Paul Gardner, Mary Frances Giles, Sokol Haxhinasto, Thomas Keown, Walter Kim, Ryan Lambert, Lisa Schad, Andrew Summey, Helen Tengkawan, Beena Thomas, and Kristi Vrooman all gave their time, energy, faith, and creativity to make this project come alive and show how "living and active" the Word of God can be (Heb. 4:12). I am deeply grateful for their generous and transparent involvement. In the end, we all wished it could have gone on for longer (albeit without beards and with bacon). A month may be long enough to pursue holiness, but it's hardly long enough to achieve it.

My sincerest thanks go to the congregation of Park Street Church, Boston, for their open ears and perseverance during four months of Leviticus sermons. I trust that the input from the

"Levites" made the listening worthwhile. And I pray that hearing made doing a reality for you too. Thanks especially for all of your encouragement and love during twenty-three years of ministry. Your openness to all the ways that Jesus makes his mark on our lives was beautiful to behold.

As for this book, I'm very grateful to Andy Crouch and the Christian Vision Project for publishing an article about this Leviticus challenge in *Christianity Today*. It generated a good deal of online conversation that was helpful in thinking through the implications of taking on Leviticus as a serious component of Christian discipleship. I also enjoyed finding out that other pastors used the article and our adventure for their own sermon illustrations, and that some even replicated the experience with their own congregations. Holiness is a worthy pursuit!

Much appreciation goes to my friend and colleague (and fellow Levite) Dr. Walter Kim, whose Old Testament proficiency contributed to the theology and approach I took to Leviticus. Thanks also to the other terrific members of the Park Street Church ministerial staff who added their own two shekels here and there. Additionally, I am indebted to the commentators and scholars whose works appear at the end, for their insights as to the meaning and application of Leviticus to ancient and modern life. Of course, all errors and bad theology belong solely to me.

You'd not be reading this were it not for Chris Park of Foundry Media, who saw the *Christianity Today* article and challenged me to turn it into a book. Her coaching and expertise in bringing this project to fruition were invaluable. Joey Paul, Holly Halverson, and Jennifer Stair at FaithWords showed faith in my words and enthusiastically made them readable. I'm so thankful for their help, editing, and direction—as well as their risk taking!

Thanks too to Kelly Lorenz for taking the photo you see on

the jacket. She's a good friend and made the most of the face I gave her to shoot.

I'm devotedly indebted to my wife, Dawn, a stellar theologian and editor in her own right. Her careful reading, suggestions, and perspective gave my feeble writing strong legs. She provided needed encouragement on days when writer's block was heavy, as well as on days when I thought the outcome wasn't worth the pixels on the screen. Her love and support contributed more than I can express.

Finally, I'd be remiss not to thank Moses and ultimately the Lord for the book of Leviticus. "Thy word is a lamp unto my feet, and a light unto my path" (Ps. 119:105 KJV).

Introduction

I was tempted to title this book *How to Be Perfct* and let the intentional misspelling convey the irony regarding the audacity of this project. Try as we might, nobody's perfect. Yet Jesus, quoting the Old Testament book of Leviticus, commands perfection (Matt. 5:48). Talk about audacity! The impossibility of human perfection leads most people to write off Leviticus as a set of idealistic virtues. Nobody can keep it, so why bother trying? The problem is that then you have to write off the Sermon on the Mount too, since so much of that derives from Leviticus.

But what if Leviticus isn't supposed to be idealistic? What if it was meant to do more than show us how much we need God's grace? What if it was written instead to show us how to live life on the other side of grace? After all, the ancient Israelites were already God's chosen people before Leviticus was written. Rather than approaching Leviticus with a view toward mitigating its commands, what if we simply obeyed them for a change?

Obedience gets a bad rap in our day. The sense is that it reduces faith to a list of dos and don'ts and discounts the relational rewards of believing in Jesus. But again, it was Jesus who said, "If you love me, you will obey what I command" (John 14:15). Obedience is part of the relationship. For Jews, and thus for Jesus, Leviticus is the pivotal book of the Hebrew Bible. It's impossible to fully comprehend such key New Testament terms as *sacrifice, atonement,* or *blood* without some understanding of Leviticus. That which Jesus cites as the second greatest commandment, "Love your neighbor as yourself," comes from Leviticus (19:18). To obey Jesus is to obey Leviticus.

But have you ever *read* Leviticus? Consider Leviticus 19:23: "And when ye shall come into the land, and shall have planted all manner of trees for food, then ye shall count the fruit thereof as uncircumcised" (KJV). What are you supposed to do with *that*?

As a Christian—as well as a longtime minister and preacher—I wanted to figure out what obeying Leviticus looked like. Not just the passage about loving my neighbor, but the parts about animal sacrifice, Sabbath keeping, skin diseases, homosexuality, stoning sinners, and dealing with mold and mildew. But given the craziness of some of these laws, shouldn't I figure out what they mean before I try to obey them? Unfortunately, Leviticus offers little by way of explanation. The best it does is mostly a divine version of "because I said so." Clearly, the only chance I had of understanding the *why* would be to *try* what Leviticus says.

I wanted to preach a sermon series on Leviticus too. As far as I knew, nobody in my congregation had ever heard one. I had one friend tell me that in his former church he had never heard a sermon from the Old Testament. However, I knew that preaching straight from Leviticus would go over like slaughtered sheep. But what if I preached a *reality* sermon series? What if I preached about the lessons learned from my actual obedience? Moreover, Leviticus was written to a chosen nation of people. It addresses what it means to be a holy *community*. What if I recruited others to join me in a month of obedience, a pursuit of the kind of holiness Leviticus teaches? My thought was to have some people obey Leviticus with me and then chronicle their experiences online, complete with pictures and videos, which I would use as sermon illustrations. And while we were at it, given the capabilities of social media, I decided we might as well post the adventure online for the World Wide Web to view and invite others outside our congregation to weigh in with their thoughts. And that's what happened.

Needless to say (but crucial to write!), a lot was learned—about Leviticus, about God, about ourselves. Some of it was assuring and some of it disturbing, yet all of it impressed on us the power of obedience as well as the necessity of grace for that obedience. In the end, we realized that God's involvement in the minutiae of human life is a remarkable reality, even if like God himself, it remains hidden from our eyes.

How to Be Perfect

Chapter One

Be Like God

Be holy because I, the LORD your God, am holy.
—Leviticus 19:2

Be perfect, therefore, as your heavenly Father is perfect.
—Matthew 5:48

When you've been preaching as long as I have, sermons can start to sound a little redundant. Christ is born every Christmas. Christ is risen every Easter. We're saved by grace most Sundays in between. I preach a lot of sermons about loving your neighbor—and some on loving your enemies. Although I like to light a little Old Testament hellfire and brimstone during the summer (with the steamy weather outside providing reinforcement), mostly I stick to the New Testament. The New Testament seems easier to understand. I typically reserve the Old Testament for Advent and Good Friday, along with some during Lent. A psalm might show up every now and then too. But I find congregations are happy enough hearing the story of Jesus over and over again.

We sometimes forget, however, that Jesus was Jewish; and

whenever he preached "the Word of God," he preached the Old Testament exclusively, since it was, after all, the *only* Testament at the time. The New Testament may seem to be easier to understand, but to fully understand what Jesus meant when he used words like *unclean* or *holy* or *blood,* you have to understand the Old Testament too. Jesus said that obedience to all of God's law can be summed up by keeping the two greatest commandments: "Love the Lord your God" and "Love your neighbor as yourself" (Matt. 22:37, 39), both of which originate in the Old Testament. The apostles Paul and James went so far as to say that to "love your neighbor as yourself" counts for loving God too (Gal. 5:14; James 2:8; 1 John 4:20–21). Surprisingly, for such an important commandment, "Love your neighbor as yourself" shows up just one place in the entire Old Testament. You find it only in the book of Leviticus (19:18).

Mention the book of Leviticus to most people, and if they have ever heard of it, what comes to mind is that arcane tome of Torah devoted primarily to the proper (and gruesome) management of sin through animal sacrifice. Others may recall mind-numbing instructions on how to rightly handle infectious skin disease and mildew, along with a mishmash of seemingly random commandments about not mixing fibers and seeds and not sleeping with your stepmother or sister or nephew—commandments deemed either pointless or plain common sense.

Leviticus is that graveyard where read-through-the-Bible-in-a-year plans go to die. Skeptics know it as ammunition for homosexual haters or as a target for animal-rights activists. Many Jews regard it as awkward and outmoded. Its unfamiliar terms and references render it irrelevant for modern readers. To slog through all twenty-seven chapters can be unbelievably tedious.

Preaching about Jesus *citing* Leviticus is one thing. Preaching Leviticus itself is something else.

PRACTICE MAKES PERFECT?

Having conveniently managed to skirt preaching from Leviticus for my entire pastoral career, I thought it might be a good idea to give it a shot. Any preacher worth his or her salt needs to tackle the difficult portions of the Bible once in a while. Besides, Christians consider the entire Bible to be inspired by God. I ran the idea of a Leviticus sermon series past some of my colleagues. They looked at me as if I were attempting sermon suicide—or worse, *homiletical homicide* (Leviticus would kill our congregation). Who'd get up on a Sunday to hear a homily on mildew?

I shared the idea with a few members of our downtown congregation. They smiled—until they realized I was serious. Then they asked me when this series was scheduled. I could tell they were making mental notes of the Sundays they'd need to plan their weekend getaways.

I asked my family what they thought. Worry writ large across their faces. Some of my female relatives who had read Leviticus remembered the bizarre assortment of cleansing rituals women had to endure as part of their menstrual cycle. What was going to be the sermon application for them? Go catch and kill a couple of pigeons each month?

Still, Leviticus is in the Bible, and in one of the most significant parts of the Bible at that. Leviticus occupies the center of the first five books of the Old Testament called the *Torah* (Hebrew for "law"). Along with Genesis and Exodus on one side, and Numbers and Deuteronomy on the other, the Torah narrates ancient Israel's story from its inception through Abraham to its arrival in the Promised Land. Leviticus works like a religious road map, detailing a long list of systematic instructions on how the people were to relate to God. This how-to list actually starts in Exodus 25 and runs through Numbers 10. It outlines the entire religious system of ancient Israel and, in doing so, reveals loads about the character of God himself (since the system is God's design).

One adjective appears over and over again throughout Leviticus: *holy*. "I am the LORD your God," Leviticus reads. "Therefore be holy, because I am holy" (11:44–45). Holiness implies ultimate purity and goodness, as well as absolute integrity and power (which clearly applies to God); but the word more literally means "uncommon" or "sacred"—that is, devoted to God. This was how holiness applied to God's people. The Lord desired that they be totally devoted to him and therefore devoted to purity and goodness.

Leviticus appears during that period in Israel's history when God traveled alongside his people in a mobile home of sorts called the tabernacle or Tent of Meeting. Having God nearby was advantageous. But it was also dangerous. Having God nearby was like living next to a nuclear power plant. You appreciate all the energy and light, but one wrong move and you're doomed. Aware of their own impurity, the people rightly feared God. Yet they needed God too. God was the source of their salvation, healing, and redemption. But how could they approach God on their own without getting blown away by his own perfect holiness?

Leviticus provides the solution. It sets up rituals, or protocols, for stepping into God's presence. You wouldn't just barge into the presence of the queen or the president without following proper protocols (unless you had a death wish). Nor would you waltz into the office of your company's CEO unannounced by his secretary (unless you had an unemployment wish). If this is true of a queen or your boss, how much more with the holy God? Leviticus established proper protocol for approaching God, complete with secretaries called priests. God picked these priests especially from a tribe descended from a son of Jacob (aka Israel) named

Levi, which included Moses and his brother Aaron (Lev. 1:7). The priestly tribe was called Levites. This is where Leviticus gets its name. *Leviticus* means "pertaining to the Levites."

The Levites mediated communication between the holy God and his imperfect people. But unlike an impervious monarch or an inaccessible CEO, God loved his people and wanted to have a personal, two-way relationship with them. The relationship God established is often called a *covenant* relationship, which worked something like a marriage (an analogy the Bible often uses). God promised to bless his people and asked only for their obedience—which admittedly to some sounds like wedlock in the worst sense. In covenant relationship, however, both obedience and blessing are motivated by love. And unlike human marriages where promises to love are made in God's name, in biblical covenants, God pledges himself ("So help me, me"). God keeps his promise to bless, and then through Jesus' obedience on our behalf, God keeps our side of the covenant too (Phil. 2:8). Thus, the obedience God asks of his people is not an obedience that earns his blessing. Rather, the blessing comes first, sparked by love, and invites obedience as a loving response. And if you don't like the word *obedience,* go with *fidelity* or better, *devotion.* After all, that's what holiness is: total devotion.

For God to invite his people to "be holy because I, the LORD your God, am holy" (Lev. 19:2), was to invite them into covenant. God set up a covenant with Abraham back in Genesis based solely on Abraham's willingness to believe God's promises of blessing. (Abraham is the representative chosen person and patriarch of all Israel.) This covenant extended to all of Abraham's descendants, the Israelites (named after Abraham's grandson Jacob, whose existence was proof positive of God's promise-keeping. See Genesis 15:1–6 and 21:1–7 for details). However, human nature being what it is, the covenant didn't hold up very well. The Israelites' screwups estranged them from God and enslaved them to the Egyptians. Then, when God valiantly rescued them from Egypt through Moses, the people showed their gratitude by building a golden cow to worship and thank instead. If you know the story of Moses, you know that the only way the covenant could go forward was for God to chisel some serious ground rules in stone. We know these ground-in-stone rules as the Ten Commandments. They were foundational to the entire Levitical system. God *chose* Israel to be his "treasured possession" and a "holy nation" (Exod. 19:5–6), but he had to *show* them how to live like the chosen and holy people they already were. He had to teach them what holiness looked like.

The somewhat random nature of Leviticus might be explained in part by the random way holiness gets taught. Imagine a toddler who grabs an electrical cord for the first time. Her parents will respond by telling her, "Don't do that again," adding the electrical cord to a lengthening list of things labeled "Do Not Touch." Whenever God's people did something unholy (wrong or threatening to the covenant relationship), it's as if God hammered on another law to keep them from doing it again. These laws pertained not only to their mistreatment of God, but also to their mistreatment of one another. God chose Israel to be a holy *nation*, not just holy individuals. Therefore, certain provisions for living together as a peaceable society were necessary—a function that law still serves in our own day. Because our tendency as individuals is to think primarily (and solely) of ourselves, something has to remind us and enforce us to consider the needs of others for the sake of the common good (or in the case of holiness, the uncommonly good). Leviticus does this by putting forth sexual ethics, household ethics, neighborhood ethics, and ethics for business, government, real estate, and law. If you lived in ancient Israel, every aspect of your communal and religious life was covered by Leviticus.

The ancient world of Leviticus differs dramatically from our own. People don't kill animals as a way of saying they're sorry anymore, yet the first seven chapters of Leviticus are about slaughtering animals and other strange ways of righting wrongs, giving thanks, and being faithful. After that come several chapters about the priesthood (which, if followed today, would make any potential clergyperson think twice before applying to seminary). Then come four finicky chapters on cleanness—everything from proper food preparation to proper skin care—which make the Lord sound terribly persnickety (apparently my mom was right; cleanliness *is* next to godliness). Following that are a couple of chapters devoted to festivals (Leviticus is the party book of the Old Testament), as well as two chapters prohibiting every type of incest and other sexual deviancy (making you wonder what the heck was going on back then). Interspersed throughout are various prohibitions against seeds and threads and a few other wacky laws that have left even the best Bible scholars scratching their heads ever since.

For the most part, Leviticus operates out of an assumed context that is left for us to deduce. For instance, Leviticus never outlines the words a priest likely spoke as he burned the sacrificial offerings. Leviticus never explains why the sacrifices often included meat, grain, and drink—though together these do comprise ingredients for a tasty menu. We do know that meals were of enormous importance in the ancient Near East, but beyond that, the meaning of these Levitical "meals" is never spelled out. No explanations appear with regard to kosher foods, banned skin infections, excess facial hair, or taboo tattoos. Why beef but not pork? Sure, a cow chews its cud (Lev. 11:3), but so what? Why does a facial blemish get you banished from the camp? Why not trim your beard? What's wrong with indelible body art? Leviticus sets laws prohibiting cross-fertilization of crops and wearing fabric blends right beside laws against spreading slander and perverting justice. Because these commands are grouped side by side, they seem to share equal importance. As far as Leviticus itself goes, they *are* of equal importance. But how are hybrid corn and poly-cotton T-shirts as bad as lying and doing harm to other people? The Lord says, "Keep all my decrees and all my laws and follow them. I am the LORD" (Lev. 19:37). But why? "Because a holy God said so" seems to be the best Leviticus offers by way of rationale.

Perhaps "God said so" is sufficient. But doesn't blind obedience to the legalities of law only turn people into legalists? Legalists follow every letter of the law out of fear of God. Maybe that's not a bad thing, except that in most cases, this fear *of* God mutates into anger *toward* God once legalists' obedience isn't rewarded the way they presume it should be (think of the older brother in Jesus' parable of the prodigal son—Luke 15:28). Legalists forget that holiness is a gift of grace that can never be earned or deserved (which is why it's called *grace*). In the New Testament book of Romans, the apostle (and former legalist) Paul writes,

> Now a righteousness [and a holiness] from God, *apart from law*, has been made known, to which the Law and the Prophets testify. This righteousness from God comes through faith in Jesus Christ to all who believe. There is no difference, for all have sinned and fall short of the glory of God, and are justified freely by his grace through the redemption that came by Christ Jesus. God presented him as a sacrifice of atonement, through faith in his blood. (3:21–25, emphasis added)

Christians interpret this to mean that God no longer relates to people vis-à-vis the law but vis-à-vis grace. Righteousness is a gift given, not a bargain struck. In Genesis, remember, Abraham was justified on account of his faith, not his obedience (Rom. 4:1–3).

In the New Testament, God is no longer the frightening, nuclear power God, but rather the father who welcomes home his wayward son before he can get a word of remorse out of his mouth (Luke 15:20). God is the generous vineyard owner who pays what he pleases, not what his laborers earn (Matt. 20:1–16). God is the good shepherd who rebuffs sensible business logic and abandons ninety-nine sheep in order to retrieve one that was lost (Luke 15:4). People are saved freely by God's grace.

All of this leads to the obvious questions: Why bother with Leviticus? Why preach a single Leviticus sermon if the law no longer applies? Because like Jesus' words, the very words Paul uses in Romans to describe grace—*righteousness, sacrifice, atonement, blood, justice, glory, redemption,* and even *grace*—are all Levitical terms! As a devout Jew and Pharisee, Paul's entire understanding of God's grace and Jesus' atoning work would have emerged out of what Leviticus taught. Ironically, preaching the book of Leviticus only teaches us *more* about grace.

JUST DO IT

I needed to preach from Leviticus. Did I dare? Had I stored up enough congregational capital to spend on an entire Leviticus sermon series? I worried that a Leviticus series could cause an exodus. Nobody wants to hear about priests burning their daughters if they become prostitutes (Lev. 21:9) or about how bodily discharges jeopardize your spiritual standing before God (Lev. 15:2). Nobody wants to know those things are even in the Bible. But they *are* in the Bible, along with prohibitions against the disabled (Lev. 21:21) and against eating most insects (Lev. 11:23). And this is all straight from God's mouth. Did you know that Leviticus contains more direct quotations from God than any other book of the Bible? That alone is reason enough to study it. Believers in God don't have the luxury to pick and choose which books to heed and which to ignore (even if this is what we do).

What would it look like to take Leviticus as seriously as Jesus did? What would it look like to take seriously all that Leviticus teaches—not just loving my neighbor, but the parts about animal sacrifices, Sabbath keeping, infectious skin diseases, homosexuality, and stoning adulterers too? *How could I preach this so that it makes any sense?* I wondered. It wouldn't work to walk through it chapter and verse. Leviticus begins harmlessly enough: "When any of you brings an offering to the LORD..." (1:2). But it goes downhill quickly from there: "Offer a male [animal] without defect" (1:3). I could envision people in the pews aghast as they thought about burning their tabbies and golden retrievers. Of course, God did not command the Israelites to kill their pets. But God did command that they kill their best livestock. What kind of God does that? And even if I managed somehow to link the deaths of countless animals to the sacrificial death of Jesus, folks would wonder why I didn't just preach about Jesus to begin with. This was going to be hard. How would I help people hear what Leviticus had to say?

I got to thinking about how the Israelites would have heard Moses preach Leviticus. Wandering through the desert, their herds and flocks in tow, indebted to a God who had delivered them from their slavery in Egypt, and now dependent on God for their lives and identity, how did *they* hear what Leviticus said? Embedded within the Hebrew word meaning "to hear" is the verb meaning "to heed" (*shama'*). As far as the Bible is concerned, to hear is to do. To obey is the way to know God. Jesus said, "Wisdom is proved right by her actions" (Matt. 11:19). These days we might call it "experiential learning." Study after study confirms that active doing rather than passive listening alone ensures higher retention and application. People learn best by doing.

This gave me an idea. If learning by doing worked for the ancient Israelites (and I know the jury is still out on that), maybe a postmodern Protestant pastor could give it a go. What better way to learn Leviticus than to live it out? Sort of like reality TV applied to church: *a reality sermon series!*

The idea came to me after reading a book titled *The Year of Living Biblically* by A. J. Jacobs (Simon & Schuster, 2007). Jacobs, a self-described agnostic Jew, decided to abide by all the strictures of Scripture as literally as possible for an entire year, just to see what would happen. I thought, *Wow, if an agnostic Jew can get a book's worth of experience out of following the Bible, how much more could somebody learn who actually believes what the Bible teaches?* If nothing else I'd get some great sermon illustrations.

I got excited just thinking about it. But unlike Jacobs, I couldn't do this alone. Leviticus was written to a community, not to discrete individuals. We tend to miss that almost every mention of "you" in the Bible is plural. The Bible commonly addresses communities, be they families, tribes, churches, or nations. Leviticus makes this especially clear: "I will walk among you and be your God, and you will be my people" (26:12). I would need to gather a community of people to do this with me.

OBEDIENCE IS A FOUR-LETTER WORD

I figured every serious Christian at least would want to *try* to obey the Bible—even the parts we don't like. Christians too easily dispense with those hard parts of the Bible Jesus himself so faithfully followed. (I know, he was Jesus, but still.) Instead of approaching Leviticus with a view toward mitigating its commands, what if we heeded them the way Jesus did (which, by the way, would mean *not* stoning adulterers, if you read John 8:1–11)? While I knew *everybody* wouldn't sign on as a participant, surely everyone would be interested in hearing the stories about those who did participate. Who wouldn't want to watch twenty-first-century American urbanites deal with the Levitical consequences of, say, a zit on your forehead? (Leviticus says you have to wash your clothes, take a bath, and shave off all your hair—oh, and slaughter three lambs.) However, I knew I couldn't get *anybody* to go along for a year. I'm not even sure I could pull off a year myself. (What this says about my own obedience is pathetically obvious.) Unlike A. J. Jacobs, I decided to shoot for a month.

But could I keep Leviticus for a month? Leviticus issues its covenant invitation: "Be holy because I, the LORD your God, am holy" (Lev. 19:2). But holiness is a tall order. Who am I kidding? Be holy like God? It's a tall order made a very *odd* order when you consider how Leviticus depicts holiness. Read Leviticus and you understand why the King James Version often translates *holy* as "peculiar." It is some weird stuff. Holiness in Leviticus has a lot to do with avoiding contamination, whether from contact with mildew or contact with menses, from eating pork or eating with pagans. "You must distinguish...between the unclean and the clean," declares the Lord (Lev. 10:10).

The fastidiousness required to adhere to Leviticus explains why Pharisees became pharisaical. It also explains why I was going to have such a difficult time convincing others to join me in my Levitical adventure, no matter how attractively I pitched it. Who wants to be a Pharisee? On the other hand, it'd be great to sing with the psalmist:

> I rejoice in following your statutes
> > as one rejoices in great riches.
> I meditate on your precepts
> > and consider your ways.
> I delight in your decrees. (Psalm 119:14–16)

To obey and be happy doing it would be huge for me. To have others join me in my happy obedience would be even huger.

I needed to sell it just right. But how? Perhaps I should appeal to a sense of adventure ("Just as the Israelites encountered God in the desert, so you too..."). Or maybe to a sense of curiosity ("Have you ever wondered how you can turn an outdoor barbecue into a worship event?"). Maybe I should take for granted that we're all Pharisees at heart and appeal to the upside of self-righteousness ("Keep the commandments and get a leg up on your backsliding brothers and sisters!"). I could appeal to Jesus' own words ("Blessed... are those who hear the word of God and obey it" (Luke 11:28). Or as a last resort, pour on the guilt ("What, nobody in this church wants to obey God for *one lousy month*?").

BUT WHAT WOULD JESUS DO?

Ironically, I expected that Jesus himself would be one of the main objections people would put up against trying to live by the book for a month. A typical response you hear whenever obedience to the law is broached is something along the lines of "Jesus fulfilled the law"—which translated means, "I'm free to disregard the law."

I conducted an informal survey at a church-sponsored barbecue luncheon one afternoon. I asked, "Given that the Bible prohibits eating pig in Leviticus 11:7, why are you eating pork?" My question was as welcome as a swarm of flies (which Leviticus also prohibits eating—11:20). The answer, as the barbecue sauce dribbled down chin after chin, was "Jesus declared all foods 'clean'" (Mark 7:19). I had to score folks points for their New Testament knowledge if not for their table manners. Still, by declaring all foods clean, Jesus was saying *not* that you can eat whatever you want, but that you can't blame your sin on what you eat. As far as we know, Jesus kept kosher.

Jesus did fulfill the law (or as the New Living Translation has Jesus saying it, "I did not come to abolish the law of Moses or the writings of the prophets. No, I came to accomplish their purpose"—Matt. 5:17). We *are* saved by grace and not by obedience. Jesus' sacrifice on the cross ended any need for further animal sacrifice for sins, and the anointing Spirit of Pentecost rendered obsolete the need for a special priesthood. But what do you do when you turn to the New Testament and discover that some of the commandments you thought you could ignore are still in force? For instance, in the book of Acts, Gentile converts are told that while they don't have to be circumcised, they should still "abstain from food sacrificed to idols, from blood, from the meat of strangled animals and from sexual immorality" (Acts 15:29). Historians argue that the prohibitions against blood were a concession to Jews who comprised most of the early Christian communities. But again, the audience in Acts 15 was Gentile. The prohibition against sexual immorality is familiar, but no rare steak? All foods may be clean, but apparently you can't eat whatever you want. Christ's fulfillment of the law was not a total exemption from keeping it.

But how do you determine what keeps getting kept? And what does suitable keeping look like? If animal sacrifice for sins and special priests are definitely out, what else is outmoded? Animal sacrifice was about more than forgiveness. Animals were sacrificed for worship, to express gratitude, and for healing too. What might that look like in twenty-first-century America? Paul goes on in Romans to say that we followers of Jesus are to offer our bodies as "living sacrifices, holy and pleasing to God" (Rom. 12:1). Sacrifices may have ended in one sense, but not in every sense. And what about "Do not cut your bodies for the dead" (Lev. 19:28)? Does that still apply? If so, how do you obey that? What *is* that? And why did the blood from guilt offerings have to be dabbed on your earlobe and big toe? What was it about your ears and toes that required special treatment? If confession and repentance are the modern equivalent of a guilt offering, should confession still involve special attention to our appendages? Since Leviticus does little by way of explaining its rationale (aside from "Because God said so"), some kind of interpretive grid for sorting out these things would be necessary.

There's little consensus among Christians regarding how to interpret Leviticus. Some people believe it should be treated as little more than ancient Israelite history. Others believe that the Old Testament law constitutes a crucial aspect of current Christian discipleship. Plenty of academic thinking has gone into arguing each side and everything in between. I wasn't going to resolve this. However, coming up with some sort of interpretive framework would provide a helpful starting point for this Levitical experiment. Our experiment might not determine the proper place of Leviticus in Christian practice, but given the practical nature of Leviticus, there was no way to begin settling how it fits into Christian practice without *practicing* it. We'd discover by doing, not by thinking about doing. Forming an interpretive grid would be a first step, but putting Leviticus into practice was the objective. It would not be enough to figure out what we think Leviticus means. We'd need to live it—which would go a long way in helping to clarify what Leviticus *really* means (and thus whether we'd need to keep on practicing it).

IS ANYTHING TOO SMALL FOR GOD?

Trying Leviticus out would be the fun part (and, as I envisioned it, the funny part too). Leviticus gets incredibly specific about the littlest things. "Examine the mildew on the walls, and if it has greenish or reddish depressions that appear to be deeper than the surface of the wall..." (14:37). I could already picture participants scouring their bathrooms and kitchens each morning while wondering why God cared so much about *kinds* of mildew. Okay, maybe this wasn't going to be so fun after all. Living Levitically was going to take time and concentration. Practically every aspect of day-to-day life would be affected.

Could it be that God really does care about *everything*? Maybe God wants our lives to slow down and be more intentional for holiness' sake. Maybe God wants us to radically transform our priorities. This is nothing new. The gospel calls for intentionality and a radical transformation of priorities too—the last go first (Mark 9:35), and the least are the greatest (Luke 9:48). The gospel teaches that God, who exists as exalted and eternal, nevertheless humbled himself in Christ to reach his people and died to take away sin and thereby make it possible to live lives worthy of our salvation. If I believe that, then I have to humble myself and die to myself too—whether that means forgiving my enemy and turning the other cheek (Matt. 5:39), letting go of my lifestyle to care for the poor (Matt. 25:37–40), or maybe even paying more attention to what I wear and what I eat.

Jesus said that you can tell a tree by its fruit (Matt. 7:20). What we believe is not what we *say* we believe. What we believe is what we do. This link between faith and deeds derives from Leviticus. God is concerned about every aspect of life because faith permeates every aspect of life. Faith is not a private matter but a public life lived. Telling a tree by its fruit implies an ability to see the fruit. If this Leviticus experiment was to be true to Leviticus, then any obedience had to be observable.

When God spoke to Moses atop Mount Sinai (after rescuing Israel from Egyptian slavery), God told him to tell the Israelites that they needed to demonstrate their favored status by their obedience (Exod. 19:3–6). The idea, I think, was so that all the other nations would see Israel's special treatment and want to be a part of it too. It's like whenever someone notices another's happiness. They want that happiness for themselves. Granted, the risk of trying to keep Leviticus, as demonstrated by the ancient Israelites themselves, is that what others witness is not the happiness of obedience but its frustrations and failures. Yet that was part of the lesson—and the reason for more grace.

SHOW AND TELL

If forming an interpretive grid was the first step, and putting Leviticus into practice was the objective, a mandatory corollary would be going public. Visibility was the only way our own congregation and anybody else could learn about Leviticus from us. They would view our fruit and our failure. Our friends, family, neighbors, and coworkers needed to notice something different—even peculiar—about us. But I didn't want to only go public locally. If we were to be "a light to the nations," as God told the Israelites they would be in Isaiah (51:4), we needed to go public globally.

What better way to go global than through the Internet? My idea was to use our church website and blog to post stories and photos for anyone to view. Yet I wanted observers to do more than merely watch. I wanted them to engage and inquire too. What about using the popular social networking site Facebook? Facebook networks you to friends from your school, work, or community and then keeps you up to speed on one another's lives, attitudes, and activities as you post them on your own Facebook page. Interests, thoughts, conversations, narratives, pictures and videos, various groups and causes—anything that can be digitized is fair game for posting on Facebook and fair game for viewing by the millions of people on Facebook. I'd have each participant open a Facebook account (if they didn't already have one) and post their exploits. I'd also create a "Living Leviticus" Face-book group for people to join so that they could comment and discuss all that we were discovering. If we learn best by actually doing, we learn second best through dialogue with those who do the doing. Facebook would provide a great platform for ongoing discussion.

Facebook would also provide a great platform for our make-shift Levitical community. Because participants in this experiment would be spread all over the place geographically (that's how it is with my urban church), being able to keep up with each other online every day through Facebook would supply a kind of *virtual* community within which to live Leviticus together. It would also supply some community oversight.

Lack of discipline was a big problem for the ancient Israelites, and certainly it would be a problem for us too. Facebook would update us on each other daily, so as long as people were honest (which Leviticus 19:11 commands), we'd know who was keeping kosher and who needed help to keep from falling off the Levitical wagon. At the same time, falling off the wagon could be as in-structive as successful obedience. Often the best lessons we learn by doing are the lessons we learn by failing. Then again, God kept the Israelites wandering the desert for forty years because all they ever did was fail—even with God himself visibly present in their midst. Learning by failing doesn't work if you never learn. Forty years? Would we be able to make it thirty days? I struggle with obedience every day. Shoot, I struggle with *wanting* to obey any day. Day One of my living Levitically would probably be fine. The novelty would be enough to get me through. But after realizing what it takes to get through one day of Leviticus, would I be able to do a Day Two? Would any of us? Or would our only success be feeling bad for being bad Christians? Would that be all the law is good for—to show us what miserable sinners we are?

If reading Leviticus succeeds only in making you feel bad for being a bad Christian, you've missed its point. Leviticus isn't in the Bible merely to show you your need for grace. It's in the Bible to show you what grace is for. The ancient Israelites were already chosen people before God laid down the law. God didn't choose Israel to be his people because he knew they could be law-abiding citizens. God chose them because he loved them. The law's purpose was not to save anybody. Rather, its purpose was to show saved people how to live a saved life. Yet even *with* grace, holiness presents plenty of challenges. In my sermons, I preach that grace gives power to live a holy life (2 Cor. 12:9). But what happens when you have the grace you need and end up screwing up just as much? It's one thing for people to feel bad about their own failed obedience. I didn't want to make them feel bad about God's grace too.

But maybe, just as failed obedience creates the need for more grace, grace itself would generate the desire for better obedience. Leviticus demonstrates the necessity for both grace *and* obedience.

Chapter Two

A Virtual Tribe of Levites

*A priest must not make himself ceremonially unclean for any of his
people who die, except for a close relative, such as his mother or father,
his son or daughter, his brother, or an unmarried sister who is dependent
on him since she has no husband—for her he may make himself unclean.*
    —Leviticus 21:1–3

As I was writing this chapter, a putrid stench filled the room. I
checked the usual suspect places—garbage cans, bathroom, closet
corners, the bottoms of my shoes—but I couldn't find the source.
A couple of days went by, and the stench intensified. Weird. The
smell was the worst right where I was working. Was my laptop
rotting? I opened my briefcase and was practically knocked over. I
found the source. A few nights prior, I had chastised my housecat
for his failure to capture a small mouse that had made its way
into our kitchen. Why did this cat think we kept him as a pet anyway? Taking the chastisement to heart, the cat not only killed the
mouse but deposited its carcass in my briefcase, where the reek of
death overwhelmed everything.

No wonder Leviticus was so opposed to coming in contact
with it. Touching a dead carcass made you unclean (Lev.

11:39–40). Death is the punishment for sin throughout Scripture, and therefore death is unholy. Consequently, coming in contact with the dead was forbidden in Leviticus, except in the case of a close relative. Family funerals would be okay, but no funerals for friends. Clearly, abiding by Leviticus was not going to be easy. How would you explain to a dead friend's family that you'd like to make the wake, but God doesn't allow it? I prayed that none of my friends would die during my Levitical month. Especially since I would need all my friends if I expected to do this Leviticus thing right.

ALL TOGETHER NOW

Any attempt at living Levitically meant living communally (or at least in the virtual sense). Leviticus was written to a nation of people, so I needed others to do this with me. Surely there were folks in our congregation itching to get more serious about holiness. The good news is that God's command to "be holy, because I am holy" (Lev. 11:44) is already kept for us by the time we finish the New Testament. Thanks to Jesus, we are *already* holy like God. Paul writes, "Once you were alienated from God and were enemies. . . . But now he has reconciled you by Christ's physical body through death to present you holy in his sight" (Col. 1:21–22). Peter calls us "a royal priesthood" and "a holy nation" (1 Pet. 2:9). Unlike for our Israelite forebears, for us holiness is no longer an unreachable ideal. This is why the Bible readily lists what holiness looks like. There's the vice-avoidance side—no lust, no greed, no revenge, no lying—as well as the virtue-added side—compassion, kindness, humility, gentleness, patience, forgiveness, love, peace, and thankfulness. So what's the problem? The problem is that despite Jesus, we lust and lie, we're mean and proud, and we don't forgive or give thanks. No wonder nobody responded to my challenge to live a month of Leviticus. We're hypocritical enough already. Why add insult to insincerity?

I tried all the previously mentioned tactics, appealing to a sense of adventure, curiosity, pride, and love for Jesus. None of that worked, so I resorted to pastoral guilt (they teach us how to do that in seminary). There are hypocrites, and then there are hypocrites who hate being hypocrites and want to do something about it. I corralled nineteen people from the latter camp to join me in this Levitical experiment, including one of my fellow ministers named Walter (we ministers are suckers for guilt).

Walter was followed by Kristen, a lawyer—appropriate given that the law is a Levitical strong suit (and lawyers wear suits). Interestingly, Kristen claimed that it was frustration rather than guilt that got her to sign on for the month. What she hates is the way Christians live in protective bubbles, with our own music and schools and books (like this one). Too much free time is spent at church with church friends. Such separateness seemed to her unhealthy and wrong. Yet, turn to the Old Testament and dang if the Torah doesn't inflate its own protective bubble to guard the Israelites from all the godless pagans surrounding them. What gives? She wrote, "The Canaanites do X (trim their beards, or whatever), so you'd better do Y just to make it extra clear that you are not them! Is this the way to live?" There was only one sure way to find out. "Sitting around and reading books on the subject is good as far as it goes," she said, "but there's another sort of understanding that comes experientially. I'm hoping that these strictures might look different when viewed from the inside."

Next to step up was Kristi, an opera singer. While there is no opera in Leviticus, living it would get dramatic (to the point that Kristi would compose an oratorio based on her experience). What convinced her to be involved was a commercial I produced to promote the project. Using a cheap Flip video camera and my trusty

PC Windows Movie Maker, I created a little digital film about what happens in Leviticus when you make a foolish promise (like the promise to obey Leviticus for a month). In Leviticus 5, it says if you make a foolish vow of any kind, whether its purpose is for good or for bad, once you realize its foolishness, you must admit your guilt and sacrifice a lamb or goat to get right with God. But if you can't afford a lamb or goat, you can kill a couple of pigeons as a penalty (5:5–7). For me, it was less a matter of affordability than convenience. My office overlooked downtown Boston and the Boston Common, where pigeons are plentiful. I lured a whole flock with a few slices of bread and got them all within reach. Having never caught a pigeon before, I underestimated their agility. As soon as I pounced, their instincts took over (as well as their wings), and I ended up on my face with a splat. I didn't catch a pigeon, though I did catch an earful from the park ranger. Nevertheless, it was funny enough to catch Kristi, and as it turned out, Brandy too.

Brandy directs a community architectural consulting firm and blames God for always doing unexpected things in her life ("Mostly awesome but sometimes very, very frustrating"). Feeling disconnected from the church community, Brandy thought that the Leviticus project might provide the kind of friendships that come with embarking on a crazy adventure together. That was definitely one of the dividends this project would pay. Journeying together toward holiness created a reliance on each other that drove us into a deeper experience of community than we would have otherwise enjoyed. Even so, Brandy worried that Leviticus might forbid salsa dancing. I assured her that Leviticus did not forbid any form of dancing. In fact, some parts of the Bible actually encourage it (Ps. 149:3).

Getting Kristi and Brandy on board meant I also got Lisa, an inner-city public school teacher. The three were best friends and already studying the Bible together, though none had ever read Leviticus. Once Lisa did read it, she admitted to being glad that "eating four-legged insects is an abomination." She'd have no trouble obeying that, though she worried that the rest might present a problem. Yet she insisted, "I can do this. I can be serious. Seriously, I can."

My pastoral guilt trip worked on a few others. Beena grew up in India and confessed how she'd always overlooked (okay, over*passed*) Leviticus and felt guilty about doing so. The same with Helen, a pharmacy student from Indonesia. Tired of having to rely so heavily on grace to alleviate her guilt, she wanted off the hamster wheel of sin-forgiveness-sin-forgiveness-sin. On the other hand, Ophera, a college professor, signed on in order to experience more of God's mercy in her life. She figured that she'd fail so miserably at keeping the Levitical law that mercy would be her only option.

At this point the group was turning out to be excessively female, something of a problem given that all Old Testament Levites were men. As women, keeping their beards trimmed would be easy, but all of the prohibitions regarding menstrual blood would knock out half the month. Recognizing the gender disparity motivated Simon to join ("We need men who will stand up to this type of public scrutiny and derision"). Simon is a network administrator who loves listening to twentieth-century serialist music loud enough to shake his cubicle walls. He said he needed a "spiritual boost" and that making "the connection between holiness and grace and the abundance of God" should do that.

Simon's enthusiasm (and evident testosterone) enticed Ian to join in. Besides needing more men, every serious twenty-first-century biblical experiment needs a video-game designer (given that 68 percent of all twenty-first-century American households play video games[1]). Upon discovering that Ian designed video games, we tried to coax him into creating sort of a virtual tabernacle where we could bring virtual cattle, sheep, and pigeons to sacrifice (surely video games could use more blood), but his theology got in the way. "Christ serves as the sacrifice that covers all sacrifices, so to speak," he wrote. "Though even if he didn't, I still don't think I'd be doing them—let's face it: I don't own a herd, and I think the authorities might be less than thrilled if they caught me throwing nets over pigeons to take them home, domesticate them, and then sacrifice them on an altar." All the more reason to design *the game,* dude. I mentioned this experiment to a rabbi friend thinking he'd be impressed with a bunch of *goyim* taking Leviticus so seriously. But instead it only got him agitated. "You're going to obey Leviticus for *a month?* What do you think Torah is? A toy to play with?" Maybe he had a point. Leviticus really isn't a game.

THE MORE, THE MERRIER

I was up to eleven people, including myself, and feeling pretty good about moving forward. But then something akin to a tipping point occurred. Call it a movement of the Spirit. Suddenly a rush of people wanted to participate. Leviticus became the rage. First came Paul, an investment manager who sought a leg up on relating to a Jewish neighbor who had moved in next door. The neighbor had asked whether Paul would mind his installing a barbecue grill in the backyard they shared. Wanting to be a good Christian, Paul offered his neighbor use of his own grill. But the neighbor, wanting to be a good Jew, demurred. He needed to install a *kosher* grill and didn't want Paul's unclean Gentile fingers even touching it. Paul thought, *Maybe if I become a Levite . . .*

Next came Kim, a dreadlocked suburban housewife who

joined on account of being a self-described Old Testament geek. Law and order caused her to feel all tingly. However, having taken a holiness inventory of her life, she concluded that while she was a good person, she hadn't yet made the holiness cut. Leviticus would help her do that. If nothing else, it would help her slow down. Its commands regarding wardrobe selection were enough to put a speed bump in her daily routine. Required to dress without mixing fabrics (Lev. 19:19), she would need to check the labels of her slacks and blouses, inevitably and drastically reducing her clothing options each morning. This was not necessarily bad news. "How much of my time is wasted on trying to figure out what to wear?" she said. "There are so many more constructive things to do, like breathe and pray, slow down in this ever-fast world. In short, fast girls aren't holy." Amen.

Sokol, our only Albanian (as well as our only scientist), signed up so he could grow a beard, something he'd wanted to do ever since he'd started shaving in elementary school. His wife said she'd divorce him if he did it, but she pulled back once he pulled rank with Leviticus 19:27: "Do not cut the hair at the sides of your head or clip off the edges of your beard." Smart woman that she is, his wife responded with Ephesians 5:25: "Husbands, love your wives, just as Christ loved the church and gave himself up for her." Sokol countered that he was only living by Leviticus (not Ephesians) for the month. Conceding, she then reminded him that Leviticus was originally lived by people roaming the Sinai wilderness. Sokol had to spend the month in the woods.

Six more people would eventually join. Thomas, a writer and an advocate for immigrants and refugees, excitedly offered his legalistic talents. He added that being on his family farm in Northern Ireland during the first week of the experiment might provide a dimension "not currently covered by the sophisticated towny folk." Andrew had devoted an entire career to all things Jewish, and his family already celebrated *Shabbat* (Jewish Sabbath) as Christians. What were a few more laws? Brian was an avid New York Jets fan who poured his life into blogging for the team (while working for IBM on the side and sleeping whenever he had a few minutes left over). He worried about his lack of discipline when it came to anything but the Jets, his worship of whom probably counted as some sort of idolatry. Mary Frances brought her Southern twang and proved to be an "all in" personality, albeit the Tennessee rather than the Texas type. As a Christian willing to write off the Old Testament, she would find simply *reading* Leviticus to be an effort in obedience. Ryan, a recent college graduate, joined because he thought it would be "cool." His main sacrifice would be toward his girlfriend and future wife. He said, "I told her that things were going to be different this month" (though he did not mention how). Finally, no Bible learning adventure would be complete without a real-time seminary student. So I recruited Christine, an Old Testament aficionado whom living by the book threatened to turn into an aficio-Pharisee. This would be a danger for all of us. *Failing* at holiness forces you to rely on grace. But what happens when you *succeed*?

We were a motley tribe of twenty whose individual attempts at keeping the law would lead to as many different outcomes as there were personalities. Yet Leviticus was not written for individuals on personal spiritual pilgrimage, but to a budding nation of nomads whom God determined to shape into a holy people. Once you get past the first chapters of Leviticus, devoted to the proper worship of God, the rest is mostly about proper treatment of your neighbor. In other words, you can't live Leviticus if you don't have others to live it with. The ancient Israelites had an advantage, if you can call it that. They were all stuck in the desert together en route to the Promised Land. They were forced to depend on each other. No way would they make it across the Jordan River without everyone working together. Leviticus is a community book.

All of us Levites lived in Boston (or thereabouts), but we weren't "together" in a proximal sense. We all lived in our own neighborhoods, in our separate domiciles, living our separate lives. None of us really *needed* the others. We came together on Sundays and occasionally other days, but Leviticus demanded an everyday sort of dependence. Andrew, I think, suggested we should all move in together for the month (easy for him, since he has four kids in his house already). Realistically, however, the best we were going to be able to do was approximate community.

Fortunately, Facebook provides pretty good tools for such approximation. It makes it possible for people to stay connected over the most mundane of life events as reported on status updates ("I'm dislodging a piece of parsley from my teeth right now"). As we were launching our experiment, Facebook was just attaining its fame (and in the minds of privacy wonks, notoriety) as a national phenomenon. We were eager to give it a ride. By befriending each other on Facebook, we could keep daily tabs on our adventures as we posted them on our walls, in notes, videos, and status updates ("I'm dislodging a piece of…um…pork from my teeth right now"). While Facebook could solve our desert dilemma, not everyone was thrilled. Mary Frances, for one, had been resisting Facebook's faddishness and intrusiveness with all her might. "I hope everyone appreciates the sacrifice I'm making for this experiment!" she wrote. "I've been fighting the one-woman war against Facebook and now I'm gonna have to cave in and join. You're killing me. *Killing* me! Alas. For my first Levitical lesson on sacrifice apparently I shall be the victim."

Among the unexpected audiences our group site attracted were clusters of observant Jews (Messianic and Orthodox) and fundamentalist Christians obsessed over whether we were following the Levitical rules rightly. I couldn't help but wonder: do people regularly type *Leviticus* into their search engines so they might police whoever might be attempting to observe its commands? In time it would feel as if we had a web-based Sanhedrin on our tails. For instance, I never realized that something I considered as benign as keeping the Sabbath could elicit such ferocious passion. Ian's mere mention that he planned to practice Sabbath on Sunday instead of Saturday brought down all kinds of Facebook fury from consternated Facebook Pharisees.

That inspired me to better explain why we were doing this, so I produced another video, creatively titled "Why We Are Doing This." In this video, I went around the table and allowed each participant to share his or her personal reasons for giving a month to Leviticus. I showed it in church and posted it on our church website and on Facebook. Aside from humorous reasons (like getting to write Levitical curses in people's birthday cards—using what you might call Leviticuss-words), the video delved into deeper motivations, which to the person had something to do with wanting to give genuine holiness a chance. We weren't taking this lightly.

WHOLE-LINESS

In searching for synonyms for *holiness,* most people opt for the phrase "set apart." Holiness has everything to do with being set apart, specifically being set apart from the profane for the sake of the sacred; that is, being set apart for God (Lev. 20:26). This is what is meant by devotion. It is unlike modern devotion, however, which typically has more to do with feelings of affection toward God, usually limited to times of corporate or personal worship ("devotions"). Unfortunately, much of our devotional life rarely makes its way beyond the pew and the private places we pray to God.

By contrast, Levitical devotion is all about an observable, public lifestyle reflective of God's holy character. A person who is devoted to God *looks like* a holy person. Holiness is a whole-body proposition—holiness holds nothing back. Just as you can't be married without a spouse, you can't be holy without God, because holiness is all about God. Even though this kind of holiness has not turned out to be a human strong suit, it remains a strong human desire—residue, perhaps, of being made in God's image (Gen. 1:26). Deep down, most of us want to be godly (or at least good) people, even to the point of lowering the standard to make it work.

With God, however, there is no lowering of standards. The reason Jesus got so angry with the Pharisees was that they adjusted their interpretations and measurements of holiness to validate the way they were already living. The supposed guardians of Torah, the Pharisees treated it like a toy for their own benefit. Jesus called them snakes and viper spawn and pretty much told them to go to hell (Matt. 23:33).

Jesus' anger in the New Testament most often manifests itself with heated words. But in the Old Testament, divine anger manifests itself mostly with just plain *heat*. In Leviticus 10, two priests overstep their priestly authority: "So fire came out from the presence of the LORD and consumed them, and they died before the LORD" (v. 2). Holiness gets hot where sin is concerned: the two do not mix. It's like those chemistry experiments you did in high school. Combine the wrong chemicals and you became toxic waste (I know this from experience). If you've read the Old Testament, you know that there is an inordinate amount of fire early on. The Israelites were always getting burned for the ways they presumed upon God's holiness—treating his favor as favoritism and as license for indulgence, corruption, and oppression of the poor. While Christians believe that Jesus' death on the cross took the heat for us (making us holy as a result), taking the heat does not let us off the burner. If anything, it turns up the heat inasmuch as to follow the crucified Jesus entails taking up our own crosses

(Mark 8:34). We're not to presume upon God's grace and treat it as permission. As with the Israelites of old, holiness still exhibits itself in an observable, public lifestyle reflective of God's holy character. Again, Jesus said you can tell a tree by its fruit. "A good tree cannot bear bad fruit, and a bad tree cannot bear good fruit. Every tree that does not bear good fruit is cut down and thrown into the fire" (Matt. 7:18–19). Oh well.

Still, God's severity is only proportionate to his love. We're never as mad as we get toward those we care about most. If God so loved the world that he gave his only Son (John 3:16), how great must be his anger toward those who reject this gift. Nevertheless, among the main purposes of God's anger, in line with his love, is to rouse people toward repentance and scare them (if that's what it takes) into covenant relationship with him, into compassionate relationship toward their neighbors, and into grateful worship (in short: a holy life). The failure to be holy is sin, sin leads to grace, and grace leads right back to holiness.

PERFECTLY PECULIAR

To be holy is to be set apart, but don't confuse being *set apart* with being *separate*. To be holy is not to be separate, but to be uncommonly different: different from those outside the community and different from the way you were when you lived life only for yourself (or again, as the King James Version renders it: "peculiar"). Of course Leviticus seems to take holiness beyond the realm of merely peculiar. Kristi read Leviticus for the first time in her life and was flabbergasted. "What was God *thinking*? What does not eating pig and not wearing mixed fibers have to do with holiness?" Only God knows for sure, but one way to get at least a hint would be to try it out. Maybe steering clear of pork and polyester had unanticipated advantages aside from lower cholesterol, smaller waistlines, and breathable clothing. Maybe obedience to the law, instead of a heavy burden, would be a joy to carry (Ps. 40:8; Rom. 7:22). If God gave Leviticus to show what he's like, there'd be no better way to be like God than to obey Leviticus—no matter how peculiar it is.

But how? Animal sacrifice and stoning adulterers are no longer allowed in America. So how to obey? And just as important, *what* to obey? I had a conversation with an Episcopal priest (whose liturgy is fashioned after Levitical liturgies right down to the vestments and the altar) and asked him what he thought about the relevance of Leviticus today. He admitted that in his mind, the only purpose of Leviticus was to shape up Israel until Jesus arrived ("The law was put in charge to lead us to Christ that we might be justified by faith"—Gal. 3:24). You'll find no mention of Leviticus in the Book of Common Prayer, aside from a mention of "Love your neighbor as yourself" (Lev. 19:18) every three years. He said that Leviticus was written for a particular time and place (by which he meant not *this* time and place).

Other pastors and theologians aren't willing to go quite so far, but they often will draw a common distinction between the *ceremonial* aspects of the law (those commands tied to the Jewish tabernacle and temple, neither of which exist any longer) and the *moral* aspects of the law (those commands tied to human behavior toward God and others who do still exist). But where does one place infections and mildew in this distinction? Or kosher diets? These can't be regarded as ceremonial since they're not temple-bound. But they're not really moral since they don't concern behaviors potentially harmful toward God or others. Okay, passing along an infection can be harmful, but rarely do we think of spreading disease as a sin. Is it? Figuring out what to obey would be almost as difficult as obeying it. Then again, the only way to figure out for sure might be simply to obey everything and see what happens. This is why I decided to leave things open-ended. If this experiment was going to work, people needed the freedom to *experiment*.

This was hard for the participants initially to accept. Given the confusion inherent to a contemporary reading of Leviticus, the budding Levites yearned for advice on what to heed and how. But I didn't want to unduly advise since (1) I could be wrong in my own take on Leviticus and (2) it would foreclose on the experiential learning aspect. An interpretive grid would be necessary, but for the most part I left it up to the participants to work that out for themselves.

HAVE YOU READ THE BOOK?

Naturally any first step required reading Leviticus, something most of us had never done all the way through. Kristi was not the only one flummoxed. Brandy confessed that her initial reaction to reading Leviticus was feeling that huge, proverbial millstone being tied around her neck (Mark 9:42). Sokol was partly to blame for this. He trundled out the *Mitzvoth,* the list of 613 commandments derived from the Torah (253 of which come from Leviticus) that Jewish rabbis created in order to summarize the law. (To this list Sokol personally added "Listening *only* to Leviticus on my iPod.") Reading the list made me feel overwhelmed too. Sokol comforted us by pointing out that we needed to feel only 41.3 percent overwhelmed, since $253 \div 613 = 0.413$ (remember, Sokol is the scientist). Keeping 41.3 percent of the commandments would be no small feat, especially when the commands include things like: Leave an unreaped corner of the field for the poor (Lev. 19:9–10; I don't farm). Do not eat fruit from a tree within three years of its planting (Lev. 19:23; who keeps count?). Do not keep a Canaanite slave forever (Lev. 25:39–43; I don't even know where to find a Canaanite). So I'm not a farmer, but how do I care for the poor? Even though I don't know the age of trees my fruit comes from, how do I honor right growing practices? Canaanite slavery no longer occurs, but how do I treat those who are indebted to me?

Some discernment would be necessary. But because discovery was such an important value in this experiment, individuals had to be left to sort out their own particular game plans on how to approach the book. It seemed a bit unorthodox, but as there's no consensus even among Jews as to what to do with Leviticus, there was plenty of room to explore. Clearly the important initial questions included whether these laws were mostly for the ancient Israelites alone. And if so, which ones and why? For some of the group, a helpful guideline was "Keep only those commandments in Leviticus that the New Testament expressly affirms." Where Jesus and Paul cited Leviticus, the commandment stood. So loving your neighbor and celebrating Passover (at least in its eucharistic forms) are definitely in, while secluding yourself from others due to a skin rash is out.

Andrew used Acts 15 as his grid. All of the first Christians were Jewish, so when an influx of Gentiles converted to Christ, the question arose as to which parts of Judaism still applied for all Christians. In Acts 15:20, 29, the Jewish Christians (James the brother of Jesus being the spokesman) met in a council and decided that Gentiles were to abstain from food sacrificed to idols; from blood (Lev. 3:17; 17:10); from the meat of strangled animals, which still contain blood (Lev. 17:13–14); and from sexual immorality (Lev. 18). Andrew took this to mean no Thai food, be careful shaving and using knives, shop at kosher markets, and refrain from sexual immorality (adultery, prostitution, and *Sports Illustrated* swimsuit calendars).

Others, wanting to stay on the safer side, decided to obey everything in Leviticus that the New Testament did not specifically nullify. Jesus declared all foods clean (Mark 7:19), so not keeping kosher was cool, but other aspects of Levitical cleanliness should be kept. Mildew, bodily discharges, and touching infected people or forbidden animals or blood were all to be avoided. Andrew wondered how anyone but the individual who did it could ever know that you touched a lizard (unclean—Lev. 11:30). Leviticus was concerned with your monitoring yourself even when you couldn't be found out otherwise. "It is God who is watching," Andrew wrote (which I wasn't sure he meant as a comfort or a threat).

Some of us would turn to Bible commentaries for help. Others would turn to Jewish friends. Mary Frances relied on a translation of Leviticus written for children. Still others went à la carte, picking commandments to try out while generally ignoring the rest. This approach drove my rabbi friend crazy. For him, the Hebrew Bible was an all-or-nothing proposition. "How can you pick and choose which parts to obey?" he asked incredulously. I assured him I had plenty of practice.

I decided to try the "dynamic equivalent" approach. In other words, choose a contemporary expression that best approximates what ancient Israelites would have done and do that. For instance, if burning grain was a way to give thanks to God each day in Leviticus, what would giving thanks daily look like now? (Okay, that's pretty obvious.) If donning a beard had something to do with marking yourself off from the pagans, how would I do that now? I thought about wearing obnoxious Jesus T-shirts for a month, but since offending pagans was not my goal, I settled instead on wearing a large cross around my neck. I don't know what pagans thought about that, but plenty of people in my predominantly Roman Catholic neighborhood took to greeting me as "Father." In Leviticus, sacrifices were offered morning, noon, and night as worship to God, so I took to sacrificing time each day and devoting it to worship too. I added an oil lamp to the mix, since Leviticus 24:2 mandates burning oil lamps.

Chris decided to try a *lectio divina* approach. *Lectio divina* (holy reading) is a monastic practice of reading Scripture contemplatively and letting God speak to you through it. She started off well, but by Day Three she heard another voice, this one from the government. She got called to jury duty. Hers was a domestic violence case, the Levitical punishment for which was at least exile (Lev. 18:28) and at worst, stoning (Lev. 20:2). Mentioning this during jury selection got her disqualified, and she got to go home early. Who says Leviticus doesn't apply today?

Wasn't this individual approach detrimental to the community emphasis of Leviticus? No, because the objective at this stage was discovery by putting Leviticus into practice, not all of us practicing the same thing. Our communal work would be sharing our experiences and their results. If in the end our discovery yielded lessons that we could apply as a community, we'd be ready to do that. Nevertheless, because Leviticus is a community book, our individual efforts often gave way to cooperation. One group of women found not working on the Sabbath easier when they made it a day of hanging out together and eating pancakes (I mean *latkes*). Others produced a creative video together on skin infections by tying it to modern American obsessions with beauty products. Still others attended synagogues and visited kosher butcheries together to get a feel for how Leviticus worked itself out in contemporary Jewish life.

WE HAVE LIFTOFF

Our assorted plans in hand, we launched on the first day of the month with fear and trembling (appropriately Levitical emotions). We each had cameras and video recorders, as well as computers on which to document our exploits. Given all that typically takes place on social networking sites, I felt as if our project was redeeming a little corner of the Internet for Jesus. But we would also be redeemed ourselves. Among the many lessons from the month, rising to the top would be the realization of how much we take God's grace for granted. Because holiness can be difficult, we default to simply admitting we're miserable sinners, get our grace, and then get on with living our lives the way we were going to live them anyway. As Ian put it, "I never before realized just how good I am at detaching God from my day-to-day life." But again, Leviticus isn't in the Bible merely to expose your need for grace. It also lays out the life that grace is for.

Yet even with grace, the best-laid plans often go awry. For Mary Frances, the end of Day One left her "fairly unimpressed with my ability to live Levitically. I've been really disappointed in myself." Kristi had to work hard to manage the guilt. Simon described how hard it was to have his sin in his face (Leviticus does have a way of pointing these things out). In fact, almost everyone found that once you step into the light of holiness, personal and communal sin cast some seriously dark shadows. Walter decided to try to keep track of his sins for a month (on paper) with the plan to burn them all at the end. After a couple of days, he understood why the sacrifices in Leviticus burned around the clock. If everybody waited until the end of the month, you'd need the fire departments of several towns to deal with the blaze.

Kim wrestled with where to draw the line: "Am I really telling the whole truth if my intentions aren't there?" Ian slipped into a sliding scale for slander (Lev. 19:16), which began with not talking behind another's back at all but ended with only saying those things about another that he deemed in his own opinion to be true. "It all sort of fell apart on me," he said. Sokol described what he felt as a "high paranoia index from day to day." Ophera moaned that keeping Leviticus was too hard and she could not do it. Thomas found being different from pagans a social nuisance. Accounting for what he was doing to his godless friends was impossible. Before the experiment, he could satisfy their curiosity about his faith with intellectual explanations about what he believed. But as soon as he started living Leviticus, they were sure he'd gone off the deep end.

While the virtual community we enjoyed did provide for day-to-day contact, it didn't replace the need we felt to be together in person. We made it a point to have (kosher) dinner together regularly (even though Jesus declared all foods clean). Again, journeying together toward holiness drove us into a deeper experience of community than we would have otherwise enjoyed. Misery loves company, especially when the misery is divinely inspired.

We decided to put our collective whining into a video called "The Challenge of Living Levitically." In it, we went around the table again, with each person describing his or her biggest difficulty with the Levitical experiment. It was a much more somber presentation than the initial video we produced. The enthusiasm everyone shared for holiness quickly gave way to collective discouragement over all of our shortcomings. In Psalm 119, we read about the writer's love of the law and how it brings him life and joy, yet our own experience was so far devoid of much joy. Brandy wondered whether she'd ever get to that joy, given how demanding Leviticus (and therefore God) could be. Brian tried not to get too disappointed, seeing his failure instead as a catalyst for leaning on Jesus. But Andrew pushed back, wondering whether we tend to use Jesus too much as a crutch and therefore miss out on the true joys of righteousness that struggling with obedience can bring.

Obviously, it was too soon to tell. Unaccustomed to such detailed demands on our obedience, we had yet to appreciate that God might genuinely desire to infiltrate every aspect of our being.

Chapter Three

Give It Up

He is to present the bull at the entrance to the Tent of Meeting before the LORD. He is to lay his hand on its head and slaughter it before the LORD.

—Leviticus 4:4

The first seven chapters of Leviticus are bloody and gruesome. Tally it up, and you have thousands upon thousands of bulls, sheep, goats, and birds killed and burned. A massive amount of blood (think the kill floor of a meatpacking plant) gets spread all over the place for a whole host of reasons. Mercifully, animal sacrifice is no longer practiced by Jews or Christians. Jews no longer do it because there's no temple in Jerusalem. Christians don't do it because Jesus' sacrifice of himself eliminated the need for any more animals to lose their lives for sinners (Heb. 10:10). Animal sacrifice is also against civil law. You can kill an animal to eat, but not to immolate.

How then is a modern-day ancient Levite to keep the Levitical law? Needless to say, it proved a real challenge. While no animals were harmed during our experiment (animal-rights activists were keeping track online), several were engaged. Given all the mention of livestock in Leviticus, it's not as if you could just ignore bulls and sheep.

Thomas didn't have to. The Levitical month returned him to his home country of Northern Ireland, where his family runs a cattle farm. Leviticus 1 commands that hands be laid on a young bull and it be slaughtered and offered to God at the entrance to the tabernacle (Lev. 1:4–5). While there was no tabernacle available in Northern Ireland (nor could there have been, since the tabernacle was replaced by the now-extinct temple), there were plenty of young bulls. But Thomas's family didn't take kindly to his idea of slaughtering one as an experiment. They were, however, happy for him to try to lay his hands on one. The bulls, on the other hoof, were not so happy about being fingered. Leviticus suggests that laying one's hand on an animal somehow transfers one's impurities to that animal. Did the bulls smell a rat?

A friend held the video camera while Thomas attempted the transfer. He approached the cattle pen carefully and warily stretched out his hand with good reason. These bulls were large animals that did not take kindly to his coaxing. "What I am finding right off," Thomas quipped, "is that cattle in ancient Israel were friendlier than those in Northern Ireland." Undeterred (especially since he was going to have to do this sixty times to comply with the twice-a-day regimen Leviticus requires), Thomas climbed *into* the pen. Perhaps sensing some serious sin, the bulls backed away, out of reach. Thomas concluded that Irish cattle must be highly selective. They were holding out for even greater sin than he could offer them. Next he tried the old bait-and-switch technique, offering a handful of feed to lure the beasts to his touch. But the cattle took no bull. Though Thomas did succeed in keeping Levitical law by locating animals without defect (Lev. 1:3), he failed to lay a pinkie of his sin on a single one. "Thank you, Jesus," he said, for saving him both from his sins and from getting gored.

While none of the rest of our tribe had access to unblemished beasts, other nondefective candidates for sacrifice were available. Simon, taking this decidedly less literal tack on animal sacrifice, came up with a list of "substitutionary bulls" to serve as his sacrifices. Simon rightly recognized that to sacrifice was to forfeit something of great value. Moreover, a substitutionary sacrifice needed to somehow stand for you (or in Simon's case, sub for his sub, since he wasn't going with the bulls Leviticus prescribed). Simon chose his nVidia GeForce2 MX 400 computer graphics card, at the time one of the best graphics cards in his collection and with no defects to boot. As an information technology professional, Simon felt this card aptly represented him and was valuable to him, making it an appropriate victim. Next came his bicycle. While not particularly valuable monetarily, it nevertheless provided Simon with transportation to and from work, and without it he'd lose very valuable time. Third was his Yamaha DGX-500 full-size electric piano. As a musician who has loved music ever since he was five, Simon plays his electric piano at weddings and other social functions as well as to soothe his soul during his darker moments. He wrote, "I cannot tell you how many little shreds my gut would turn into if I were to put it on the chopping block."

The conditional tense of that last sentence accurately indicates what did not happen. No fire consumed Simon's substitutionary bulls. He couldn't bring himself to burn them (though he said the real problem was that he couldn't figure out *where* to burn them since any fire big enough to consume all this equipment would surely have summoned the local fire department). Committed to burning *something,* Simon turned to Leviticus 2 and the instructions on grain offerings. Animal sacrifices rendered a person acceptable to God. Grain offerings expressed gratitude for the acceptance. With the grain offering, a worshiper acknowledged that all good things belong to and come from God. By giving back a portion, a worshiper gives thanks for God's provision. This same rationale applies to passing the plate in church. We give back to God a portion of what was given to us (after we pay our taxes—we still have to render unto Caesar what is Caesar's—Mark 12:17).

Leviticus says that the grain offering "is to be of fine flour. He is to pour oil on it, put incense on it...and burn this...an offering made by fire, an aroma pleasing to the LORD" (2:1–2). So Simon grabbed a pan and then went to the cupboard and located a bag of all-purpose flour. He then retrieved a bottle of extra-virgin olive oil, but unable to locate any incense to go along with it, he decided to substitute sesame seed oil, reasoning that it was aromatic enough to do the trick. (After substituting graphics cards for bulls and now sesame oil for incense, we took to calling him Substitutionary Simon. Though in fairness, Leviticus 2:7 says if you're cooking your grain offering in a pan, you can leave out the incense.) Short an altar too, Simon went with his stove. He mixed the ingredients together in a pan and started cooking.

At first the aroma was quite pleasing (as Leviticus said it would be), but in a matter of minutes the mixture browned and the scent it gave off smelled more like burning popcorn and newspaper. The smoldering mixture also started spewing a ton of smoke, forcing Simon to throw open all the windows in his tiny apartment to air the place out. Thankfully, no one dialed 911. As it was, the stench got all over his clothes, making him smell like burnt toast for the rest of the day—which included a business flight he almost missed because he was cleaning up after his grain offering. Cramped in coach class, his "pleasing aroma" elicited grimaces and stares from the other passengers seated nearby. There was no word on how officers reacted to the way he smelled when he went through security. For Simon, the stench seared into his senses the all-consuming demands God lays out in Leviticus.

Did Simon's overcooked grain offering bring him closer to heaven (aside from his taking the odor with him up thirty-five thousand feet)? It's as hard to say as it was to do. I imagine sacrifices were accompanied by mixed emotions, resentment sometimes among them. Why does God require my best produce and livestock? It's not as if he has to eat. Why must my hard-earned possessions be burned up? Couldn't they at least be collected and given to people in need? And why must I do this every day? Imagine what it must have been like walking into the tabernacle, where the sacrifices occurred, and watching your precious assets go up in smoke day after day. The acrid smell of blood, burning flesh, and scorched grain reinforced what must have seemed at times like a total waste. Yet to God, the stench was a pleasing aroma because it represented the total devotion of holiness. In both the Old Testament and the New, the Lord asks his people to give themselves to him fully—heart, mind, soul, and strength (Deut. 6:4–5; Mark 12:30). Jesus said following him meant losing your life in order to save it (Mark 8:35). The Bible sets up faith as an all-or-nothing proposition, and nothing symbolizes totality more than fire.

In return, the Lord promised his presence and with it security, identity, daily bread, and deep joy. Envision walking into the tabernacle, where you watched your most valuable belongings go up in smoke, but then imagine God appearing as he appeared to the Israelites, in a fiery cloud of smoke that engulfed the tabernacle. He met their smoke with his smoke. It was a powerful connection. If you've ever experienced such a connection with God, you'd give anything for it never to end.

U-HAUL HOLINESS

In Exodus 25, the Lord instructed Moses to construct the tabernacle, a dwelling place for God and a meeting place for him and his people (*tabernacle* means "dwelling place"). The tabernacle functioned as a bit of heaven on earth, which explains why its building plans were so extensive and precise. It was intended to look like heaven. However, it also had to be portable enough to travel with the Israelites across the Sinai desert on their way to the Promised Land. So Moses made what became God's mobile home, replete with a living room (Holy of Holies), a dining room (Altar of Presence), a kitchen (bronze altar), and a bath basin. In the Holy of Holies sat the mercy seat atop the ark of the covenant, which contained the Ten Commandments, those ground rules for the covenant between God and his people. As long as Israel kept covenant, God would keep blessing them with everything they needed and then some. Break the covenant, and things got pretty dicey. The good news was that God's blessings provided sufficient incentive for good behavior (grace does that). The bad news was that the Israelites weren't easily incentivized. It was like trying to pay your children to play nice. It only works for so long.

Playing nice all the time can get awfully boring—especially when coupled with hiking forty years across barren desert. Toss in one temptation after another (the pagan kids across the street who get to do whatever they want), and you have a recipe for disaster. Something was bound to go wrong, and it did, over and over again. The Israelites were notorious for taking God's presence for granted. They presumed his favor to be permission to do as they pleased. The worst was the way their heads so easily turned to chase after idols, the material gods worshiped by the various cultures they encountered en route.

Idolatry can be hard to understand in modern times. Crafting deities out of wood or metal seems silly. Yet look around today and see how easily people idolize the shiny metal and fancy wooden things in their lives, be they cars, houses, electronic gadgets, or gizmos—in addition to the enticing idols we've made out of money, power, and celebrity.

All sorts of things can be turned into idols. One day into her Levitical month, Mary Frances wrote that she got a "sneaking suspicion that my time is my idol. I hold it, hoard it so selfishly." It became evident that she loved to keep her time for herself more than give it to God. She'd planned to spend the first Levitical day reading and praying over the first few chapters of Leviticus. But her plan came to a screeching halt when she woke up late and quickly found a few other "necessary" things to do. When she decided to put off her reading until the tasks were completed, her day soon unraveled into lots of errands that, in the end, kept her from doing the very thing she devoted herself to the month to accomplish—namely, make more room for God. "Here I sit, well past midnight with not much to show for it, finding myself terribly unprepared for this endeavor."

The tabernacle was designed to confront idolatry as well as all the other ways the Israelites snubbed God. On the one hand, constructing an enormous mobile home for God seems downright nutty. "The God who made the world and everything in it is the Lord of heaven and earth and does not live in temples built by hands" (Acts 17:24). Yet somehow the tangibility of the tabernacle (with its size and scent and smokiness) made the presence of God *more* real than it otherwise might have seemed. And the more real God's presence seems, the less likely one is to seek alternatives. After all, God's presence is the *par excellence* expression of his pleasure (Exod. 33:15–16). Therefore Mary Frances decided that the best way to combat her idolatry and experience God's pleasure was to construct a tabernacle in her apartment ("I will put my dwelling place among you"—Lev. 26:11). It would not mimic the original tabernacle in biblical proportion (those specs are in the book of Exodus anyway), but in proportion to the space she had available (four hundred square feet of apartment), her tabernacle would seem just as enormous.

She did try to come as close as she could to the Levitical model. Possessing neither ram's skin nor a porpoise skin for the roof and sides, she made do with a light blue (porpoise-colored) sheet and a red fleece (ram-textured) blanket. Inside her rendition of the Holy of Holies was her fireplace, since fire codes wouldn't allow open flames anywhere else ("Sorry it's so dirty in there, God!"). She set it up with a makeshift altar of incense (some fragrant oil and incense sticks), a lampstand (a candlestick and a few candles), a curtain to cover the Holy Place (some purple fabric), and a basin of water to wash with (and to put out any fires that got out of hand). In Leviticus, only priests were allowed in the Holy Fireplace, but because of Jesus, Mary Frances reckoned that any who believed in Jesus constituted a part of a "royal priesthood" (1 Pet. 2:9) and were thus welcome to enter her tabernacle (albeit a few at a time).

She also added a couple of things that didn't appear in the biblical blueprints: paper and a pen and a large map of Tennessee. The paper and pen were for writing down her sins so she could burn them (as Walter did, sort of like atonement without the bloodshed). The map became part of her tabernacle because it was really big and she had no other place for it; plus, she thought it could serve as a good reminder of what the Promised Land is like (remember that Mary Frances is from Tennessee, a place that she would describe as "God's country"). She invited folks to "come on over during normal business hours and 'sit a spell' in my tabernacle. You can come and pray, write your sins or idols or offerings to God on the papers, and then burn them in the Holy Fireplace and dream about good ol' Rocky Top" (another Tennessee thing).

We were all extremely impressed by Mary Frances's industriousness and creativity. Kristi, however, couldn't help but be envious. She confessed that Mary Frances's tabernacle caused her to covet, which was in direct violation of the tenth commandment ("Not only am I terribly envious over what you've done, but I'm now also fighting feelings of inadequacy"). Kristi never made it to Mary Frances's tabernacle to write down her envy and burn it. Ironically, this may have been a good thing. Kristi would have been tempted to burn down the tabernacle too. Covetousness can turn very destructive.

Yet even with her architectural ingenuity, Mary Frances never witnessed a cloud descending from heaven to envelop her apartment (though she did get nervous one unusually foggy morning). In Leviticus, the smoky cloud that covered the tabernacle indicated the Lord was home, but it also worked as a kind of veil since no one could see God and live (Exod. 33:20). Though God desired a relationship with his people, nobody was allowed casual entry into his presence. Holiness (God) could not tolerate the presence of unholiness (impure people) and remain holy any more than a sterilized operating room can tolerate the presence of a single germ and remain sterile. It's not that the Lord was some sort of neat freak (though reading through the cleanliness chapters in Leviticus does make you wonder about that), but God was a freak for justice, integrity, loyalty, love, and honesty, all of which are essential characteristics of his nature. To the extent that these were *not* characteristics of a person's nature, approaching God became a risky proposition. To borrow another analogy, it was as risky as standing before a judge when you both know you committed the crime.

SCARED STRAIGHT

Due to the ease with which people approach God in our day (whether in prayer or nonchalant conversation), it's hard to appreciate the terror caused by God's proximity in ancient Israel. Maybe if we encountered more smoke and thunder, we'd be more deferential. Back then, even without the pyrotechnics, fear of the Lord was common and encouraged (Lev. 25:17). This fear was not so much dread of God's punishment against wrongdoing as it was awe of God's might. Therefore fear was not a reason to stay away from God. Rather, fear ensured that you approached God with due respect and humility, eager for the relationship he offered, but eager to do it right.

The Bible frequently describes our covenant relationship with God as a marriage (Jer. 3:14; 31:32; Isa. 54:5; Hosea 2:19–20; John 3:29; Rev. 21:9). Most marrying people want to do it well, which means making sacrifices for the sake of the other person. Spouses will sometimes whine about sacrifice, but there's no way to have a good relationship without it. In Leviticus, sacrifice didn't whine, but it did moo, bleat, and chirp. Bulls, sheep, and birds comprised the burnt offering, the first sacrifice mentioned in Leviticus (1:2). The title sounds a little redundant (all sacrifices were burnt), but unlike the others, which allowed leftovers, the burnt offering was burnt to a crisp. This complete *consummation* (in both the conflagrant and conjugal senses of that word) signified complete covenant commitment on both parties' parts. The burnt offering was also the only one offered at the door of the tabernacle instead of inside. It functioned like your admission ticket into God's presence. (Mary Frances opted out of doing burnt offerings, since it would mean burning meat in the hallway of her apartment building. She wanted to get into God's graces, but she also needed to stay in her landlord's graces.)

The burnt offering wasn't cheap. It cost you a perfect bull from your herd. However, if you couldn't afford a bull, you could offer a sheep or a bird. God made sure that everyone could gain access to him regardless of economic status. You needed to sacrifice; you didn't have to go broke to do it. Moreover, you couldn't go out into the desert and trap a wild bull or go onto the Boston Common and grab a pigeon. Whatever you gave had to be yours to give. It had to cost you. In the book of 2 Samuel, a guy named Araunah tried to give King David a free ox for his burnt offering, but David refused the gift. He said, "I will not sacrifice to the LORD my God burnt offerings that cost me nothing" (2 Sam. 24:24). So David paid Araunah the hefty sum of fifty pieces of silver.

As a pricey admission, the burnt offering was sort of like a ticket to the Super Bowl or a U2 concert. Even tickets for bad seats can go for hundreds of dollars (and you still have to enter a lottery for the opportunity to buy them). For me and most of my friends, such an outlay represents a significant chunk of our paychecks. But here's the thing: some of those friends (the crazed football or U2 fans) would pay it gladly. It worked the same way for the Israelites. Their enthusiasm for meeting with God would be like our enthusiasm for meeting Tom Brady or Bono (as sad a commentary on us as that is). To cough up prized livestock to do it was worth the price. With God you got your sins forgiven, your prayers heard, and his love for you affirmed. It made for a happy day—both for you and for God (It is "an aroma pleasing to the LORD"—Lev. 1:9, 13, 17).

BARBECUED BLESSEDNESS

Now it wasn't the smell of burning meat that made God happy (as sweet smelling as barbecue can be). Like the smoke of total

devotion, it was the aroma of atonement that brought God pleasure. When we think of atonement, we tend to think of it solely in
terms of taking away sin. But in Leviticus, atonement covers the
whole range of reconciliation. If human sin is as bad as the Bible
portrays it, burning any one bull or sheep to cover it seems somewhat far-fetched. More was required. The Hebrew word translated "atonement" (*kaphar*), used almost fifty times in Leviticus,
does mean "to cover or cleanse," but it also means "to appease."
Because the burnt offering was offered with no particular sin in
mind (that kind of atonement is restricted to sin and guilt offerings), it was viewed as a gift given in order to pave the way for
a better relationship. You see this sort of thing in diplomatic ne-
gotiations where two parties often start by exchanging gifts. The
difference is that with God, people approach him from a severely
disadvantaged position. He's holy; we're not even close. Sacrifice
both acknowledged the distance and sought to bridge it. This
brought great pleasure to God, the same pleasure we experience
whenever a person from whom we've been estranged offers an
apology or makes amends.

The Hebrew word translated as sacrificial "offering" (*qorbān*)
comes from the verb meaning "to bring near" (*qārab*). But because we equate sacrifice so often with giving up, we often miss
its deeper meaning. Giving up elicits feelings of resentment and
depravation. You give up chocolate for Lent and all you can think
about is the chocolate you're not eating. You give up going to
the beach for going to church and all you do is think about sand
and sun during the sermon. Leviticus thwarts such psychology by
emphasizing sacrifice not as giving *up*, but as giving *to*. Instead of
depravation leading to resentment, sacrifice puts its focus on generosity and humility for the sake of embrace. *Giving to* accentuates
the recipient, thereby bringing joy to receiver and giver alike.
"God loves a cheerful giver" (2 Cor. 9:7). So does everybody. Give

fine chocolate to your wife, and it makes everybody happy—and her forgiveness more likely (if, by chance, you've done anything wrong, which you probably have).

One of the more endearing stories in the Bible is about a prostitute who breaks open a jar of expensive perfume and lavishly pours it over the head and feet of Jesus (Luke 7:37–50). A comparable gesture in our day might be providing Jesus with a luxury car to keep him from having to walk so much. Those who witnessed the woman's extravagance became indignant, mostly because they knew this woman's reputation. However, Jesus met her costly and loving gesture with his costly and loving grace, recognizing her sacrifice as an offer of repentance and a desire to draw near to God again.

In Leviticus, it's not expensive perfume that gets poured out, but blood—and lots of it. God decreed, "It is the blood that makes atonement for one's life" (Lev. 17:11). Due to the need, the burnt offering was made three times a day. The people pooled their livestock and hauled a representative bull or bulls to the tabernacle every morning, noon, and night (given the massive outlay, sacrifices and offerings had to be corporate affairs to prevent nationwide starvation).

Despite the enormous amount of blood, not a drop of it made the Israelites any more God's chosen people than they were before they burned their bulls. God *chose* Israel of his own loving free will; they had no say in his choosing. God rescued them out of their brutal slavery in Egypt, making them his bride before they ever got to Mount Sinai, where Moses got the law. It was by God's grace they were saved (just as in the rest of the Bible—Eph. 2:8). God gave the law to show them what a saved life looked like and to help them make things right when they screwed up. At this point, a Facebook reader from Sweden wrote to bemoan the way that *Torah* always gets translated as "law," especially given all of the disagreeable associations that *law* generates. She pointed out how *torah* actually derives from a Hebrew root meaning "to shoot an arrow," which is about shooting straight and true. It has to do with pointing the right way or directing along the right path. The law was the key to the good life; thus, the psalmist would sing, "I love your commands more than gold, more than pure gold, and because I consider all your precepts right, I hate every wrong path" (Ps. 119:127–128).

Walter responded that the sentiments of the psalmist are not always his own. *Love* and *law* do not typically come as a matched set. *Love* was not a word many of us modern-day Levites used to describe our month of living Levitically. Walter wrote,

> If anything, the attempt to live Leviticus is invasively convicting. Its stipulations touch upon virtually every conceivable arena of life—from base, bodily functions to austere religious disciplines. Trying to keep up is daunting, and indeed, impossible. I had the intention of reading one chapter a day and seeking to apply one thing from that chapter for that day. Well, I failed. The cumulative effect of each day was too much. So, initially, it appears that the lesson is: holiness is way too big for me.

Eventually, however, Walter discovered the law's power to elicit love and joy. He observed how *lex* (the Latin word for "law") is like *sex*. Both are not about good techniques but about a covenantal relationship (again, back to the marital connection). Just as good sex can keep a marriage strong, so good *lex* keeps your relationship with God strong. And just like good sex in a marriage, good *lex* can make for great joy—as the psalmist sang. Since grace came first, Walter observed, "Obedience is not something I've *got* to do, but something I *get* to do. If I find the law to be an onerous killjoy, then maybe this is a clue that I have lost sight of the Lawgiver."

FINE DINING

Yet when you think of all the blood that the law requires, especially when it wasn't required to save you, you still have to ask: Why do it? Why was the Lawgiver bent on having his people slaughter so many animals? Why all the fire? Again, Leviticus offers little by way of rationale, aside from "The LORD said so." But when you look at the sacrifices themselves—meat, grain, drink by candlelight—doesn't that sound an awful lot like a fancy dinner menu? Except for the burnt offering and a small representative portion from the others, none of the sacrifices were *burned* as much as they were *cooked*. Your gift to God gave back to you. It fed you dinner, or more specifically, it fed the priests dinner. In Leviticus 7:28–36, God reserves the breast meat for Aaron and his sons; the rest of the priests got dark meat. Like ministers paid by congregations in our day, this was how the Levites earned their bread (or more specifically, their meat).

As for the animals themselves, Kim was heading home from church after the Leviticus month had ended when Emilia, her five-year-old daughter, asked, "Do animals go to heaven?" Kim wrestled to remember how she answered the question back when her ten-year-old daughter, Ella, asked it. But then Ella beat her to it.

"Absolutely," Ella replied. "Animals definitely go to heaven."

Kim thought her own answer many years prior must have made quite an impact for Ella to respond so emphatically, so Kim asked her to elaborate.

"God wanted the Levites to sacrifice animals, remember?" Ella said. "Do you *really* think he would ask them to do that if the animals were not going to a better place?"

Childlike faith notwithstanding, Leviticus says nothing as to the heavenly destination of animals. But that they ended up as food to eat is not a *bad* destination, at least not biblically speaking (see Psalm 104 for a litany of food from the earth that graciously God provides). Nutritionally speaking, food sustains life. But *how* we eat matters too. In the ancient Near East, meals were of enormous importance. They served as a means of celebrating (a holiday feast), conducting business (over lunch), making peace (over a candlelit dinner), or simply catching up (over break-fast)—all the while nourishing you and keeping you alive. Levitical sacrifices did this too. Those disturbed by animal sacrifice in the Bible can take comfort that most of these animals were killed for food. By tying food to sacrifice, Leviticus made meals into worship (and vice versa), a reality played out through the Bible from Passover to the Lord's Supper to the long-awaited Wedding Feast of the Lamb (Rev. 19:9).

FLESH EATERS

Understanding Leviticus this way helps explain one of the other weirder passages of Scripture found in John's Gospel. Jesus said, "I tell you the truth...whoever eats my flesh and drinks my blood has eternal life, and I will raise him up at the last day. For my flesh is real food and my blood is real drink" (John 6:53–55). Jesus clearly speaks metaphorically (a better translation than "real" would be "true"; cf. NRSV, NASB). In Mark 14:25 (as well as Matt. 26:29 and Luke 22:18), Jesus calls the cup "the fruit of the vine," acknowledging that its contents are not literally his blood. However, the odd nature of the metaphor has given rise to everything from accusations of Christian cannibalism to the long-standing Roman Catholic doctrine of transubstantiation (whereby the bread and wine of the Eucharist are believed to become the actual flesh and blood of Jesus). We read Jesus described in John's Gospel as "the Lamb of God, who takes away the sin of the world" (1:29), and we know from Leviticus that a lamb takes away sin by shedding its blood (Lev. 3:7–8; 4:32–34). Yet in accordance with Levitical practice, the lamb not only atones but nourishes. (Fortunately for Communion preparers ever since, Jesus did not take a lamb shank and say, "This is my body.") To "eat and drink" Jesus is not a reference to cannibalism or to the mystical transformation of bread and wine, but to Jesus' role as Levitical sacrifice. Jesus provides access to God, atones for sin, and feeds us with his flesh, "the bread of life" (John 6:48).

Why did Jesus tie his death to Passover rather than to, say, Yom Kippur, the Day of Atonement (Lev. 16)? It seems that Jesus intended to make the further point that his sacrifice not only nourished and saved, but kept safe too. In Exodus, as God readied to unleash his wrath against Egyptian cruelty—indeed, against all human wickedness—the Israelites were instructed to smear lamb's blood on their door frames as a safeguard against God's destructive plague (Exod. 12:12–13). Likewise, Christ's blood safeguards God's people from the wrath to come, when all injustice and oppression and tyranny will be dealt with for good (1 Cor. 5:7).

Given this connection, you'd expect Jesus to instruct that the disciples smear his blood on their foreheads. But instead Jesus tells them to *drink it*. This is a problem as far as Leviticus goes.

Leviticus prohibits consuming or even touching blood. The reason is also found in Leviticus 17:11—namely, that blood is life and all life ultimately belongs to God, the source of life. The blood drained from animals (never eaten) was splattered against the sides of the altar in recognition of this reality. This explains how "it is the blood that makes atonement" (Lev. 17:11). If the paycheck for sin is death (Rom. 6:23), then the payback to God is blood for the life that was lost. Life pays for life (Lev. 24:18). It is only with blood that the lost life can be redeemed. Without the shedding of blood, there is no forgiveness (Lev. 4:20; Heb. 9:22). (Some Jewish scholars add that the payback in Leviticus 17 is also for taking the life of an animal to be eaten. Because all blood is sacred, killing a bull for dinner entails giving the blood back to God for taking the blood from the bull.) This separation of blood from the body explains the language of the Lord's Supper. Jesus speaks of "my body" and "my blood," as opposed to, say, "my flesh and bones" or "my heart and soul." But it still doesn't explain why Jesus would say, *"Drink* my blood" (forget cannibalism; we're in the realm of vampires now).

Jesus does something radically new, which may be one reason he calls it the "new covenant in my blood" (Luke 22:20). Rather than thinking of the blood of atonement only in terms of taking *away* sin, Jesus seems to be adding the idea of atonement as taking *on* life, specifically taking on *his* life. Speaking of his resurrection, Jesus said, "Because I live, you also will live. On that day you will realize that I am in my Father, and you are in me, and *I am in you*" (John 14:19–20, emphasis added). Instead of blood as life *for* life, Jesus introduces his blood as life *in* life. This does square with the Levitical assertion that life is in the blood (17:11). Only now, it is *Jesus' life* that is in the blood, a life that we are not to avoid but eagerly imbibe. Having saved us from death by shedding his blood, he gives us new life by our drinking his blood (metaphorically speaking, that is). To give blood is to give life.

TAKE IT TO THE BLOOD BANK

"Give life" is a phrase you see blazoned across advertisements for the Red Cross Bloodmobile. Kristen signed up at her work when the Bloodmobile made its annual stop during the Leviticus month. ("I am a 'hard stick' as they say in the vampire business, and the nice people in the Bloodmobile outside had to make a couple of attempts before I started gushing. Ow.") She reflected on Leviticus over juice and cookies after having some life drained from her arm. While she wouldn't go as far as describing donating blood in terms of atonement (that language is reserved for God), she did describe it in terms of giving part of herself for the sake of another. "Blood is holy—and is there to be shed so that others might live. We gratefully receive life and health from blood that was shed for us, and in joyous response we offer ourselves as the body of Christ to be broken and poured out for the world. Rarely do we get to live that out quite so literally."

As with Jesus (and to a much lesser extent with Kristen), to give blood is to give a most precious thing. And as far as Kristen and other blood donors go, you never know who will be the recipient. But what you do know is that your gift will be unconditionally received. This is part of what makes donating blood so rewarding. In relation to the Levitical sacrifices, God's total acceptance of the sacrificial gifts signaled his total acceptance of the giver, an acceptance guaranteed before the worshiper stepped foot into the tabernacle. It was this unmerited acceptance that made *giving to* God so joyful. It's also what motivated a desire to *give back.*

The sacrificial system that foreshadowed the ultimate sacrifice of Jesus for sinners also foreshadowed the sacrifice of Christians too. Only rather than giving an animal, we're invited to give ourselves. "In view of God's mercy," the apostle Paul wrote to the Romans, "... offer your bodies as living sacrifices, holy and pleasing to God" (Rom. 12:1). This is burnt offering language (Lev. 1:3)—total acceptance on the part of God, which beckons total giving back on the part of the worshiper. What does this total giveback look like? It looks like Leviticus: honoring God with every fiber of your clothing, every cell of your skin, every morsel on your plate, every hour of your work, every moment of your rest; all your responsibilities, all your relationships, everything totally devoted to God.

DEVOTION AS DONATION

Some Christians take this more literally than we did. I served on a hospital bioethics committee where the issue of organ donation came up during the Levitical month, particularly as donation related to altruism. There was the case of a Christian woman who believed that the Bible's call to love her neighbor as herself out of a total and sacrificial commitment to God could be obeyed by freely giving one of her kidneys to a stranger. In doing so she would be doing to others as she would want done to herself, just as Jesus said (Matt. 7:12; where Jesus added, "This sums up the Law and the Prophets").

The ethicist who presented this case to us was nonplussed. He had asked the woman, "Are you aware that there is a possibility you could die?"

She replied, "I believe God wants me to use my life to help other people, and the rewards will be a much deeper happiness and a sense of real fulfillment. Many people are willing to kill for what they believe in; why not allow people to take risks to save a life?"

The doctor, finding out that this woman was a mother, then asked, "Have you considered that if anything goes wrong, your seven-year-old son would not have a mother?"

She replied, "What about police and firemen? Should they not do their jobs because if something happens to them, their children will have one less parent? The best I can do for my son is give him a good example. If I die, he will still have a loving, dedicated father."

With Leviticus swimming around my brain, I was struck by what I perceived to be a reasonable, straightforward, and sacrificial faith. Whether most of us would ever do this (and I'm guessing the answer is no), this Christian woman's altruism still looked to me like a genuine and overwhelming act of Christian love and obedience.

Yet to the presenting ethicist and others, her altruism was flagrantly unethical. "How dare a perfectly healthy person offer her kidney to a stranger!" "How can we believe her motives are pure?" "Her religion was compelling her to do it."

Now I was the one who was nonplussed. Granted, Jesus does not say we must give our kidneys to strangers. There is cause for being suspicious of anyone's motives inasmuch as all human motives warrant suspicion. But that this woman did go on to donate her kidney to a dying Texas man and saved his life at a personal cost to herself demonstrated a powerful example of sacrificial love at work.

The grace that saves is the grace that suffers for others. Was this woman's sacrifice of her kidney crazy and *peculiar*? Absolutely, but such is the nature of grace and the nature of holiness. Their inherent peculiarity is why grace and holiness are met with such resistance. Thus Christians should never be surprised when our own obedience is met with resistance and persecution too. In fact, if your own obedience is *not* met with resistance and persecution, you might want to reconsider your obedience.

Chapter Four

Bad Skin as Sin

When a person has on the skin of his body a swelling or an eruption or a spot, and it turns into a case of leprous disease on the skin of his body, then he shall be brought to Aaron the priest or to one of his sons the priests, and the priest shall examine the diseased area on the skin of his body. And if the hair in the diseased area has turned white and the disease appears to be deeper than the skin of his body, it is a case of leprous disease. When the priest has examined him, he shall pronounce him unclean.

—Leviticus 13:2–3 ESV

Leviticus takes bad skin very seriously. For two entire chapters (13 and 14, the longest chapters in the book), God goes on and on about all kinds of skin conditions from a rash to a pus-spewing sore. Getting a hive or a boil got you banished from God's presence and run out of town. Get a zit, and Leviticus dictated that you tear your clothes, tousle your hair, cover your mouth, and scream "Unclean!" as you made your way out to the city limits (Lev. 13:45). Ancient Israel would have been a nightmare for teenagers. It was a bad place to be sick at all.

During the first week of our Levitical month, I came down

with a nasty head cold (not a skin infection, mind you, but just as infectious). I didn't think to tear my clothes or muss my hair, though I probably looked as if I had. I did, however, remember to cover my mouth whenever I sneezed. It's one of those things we're taught to do early on—who knew that it came from Leviticus? Kristen observed how most people say "Bless you" when you sneeze. But she also knows someone who says, "May the demons leave your body!" There seems to be an inherent association between sickness and evil. My friends, confronted by my mucus-spewing state, went so far as to flash me that cross-shaped finger gesture that people typically reserve to ward off evil.

While teaching us to cover our mouths whenever we sneeze, our mothers also taught us to wash our hands afterward: "Wash your hands and say your prayers; germs, like Jesus, are everywhere." Leviticus commands you to wash not only your hands, but the rest of your body and your clothes too. The same goes for the person you sneeze on, as well as anything you touch. Once bathed and cleaned, you then must wait seven days, after which you take another bath and take two sacrificial birds to the tabernacle, one for a sin offering and the other for the burnt offering (Lev. 15:1–15). My mom always told me, "Cleanliness is next to godliness," but Leviticus carries cleanliness to a whole other level. In Leviticus, cleanliness is not *next to* godliness but appears *to be* godliness itself. Being clean in Leviticus applies not only to what you discharge and spew, but also to where you live, what you wear, and what you chew. It's all very serious (and tedious) business.

BEAUTY IS A BEAST

In hygienically hyped, skin-obsessed America, living Levitically with our skin should have been easier. Yet despite a treasure trove of health and beauty aids at our disposal, keeping smooth skin for a month was no day at the spa. For assistance, Kristi and Mary Frances headed to the mall and to Sephora, the epitome of all things skin care. Though expecting to find every kind of product for perfect skin, they were not expecting these products to be gorgeously labeled as theological virtues (apparently someone in the marketing department at Sephora had been reading Leviticus too). *Grace* and *Hope* and *Purity* came packaged in jars promoting relief for the driest and most sensitive hide. *Virtue* could be bought as a shower gel, lotion, cleanser, moisturizer, exfoliator, clarifying toner, purifying oil, and radiance oxygenating serum (no wonder skin gets referred to as *complex*ion). However, on the off chance that actual skincare products failed to keep their promises, the Internet offered other options: Perfectskinphoto.com is a software package that automatically removes zits, wrinkles, cellulite, snot, and unwanted facial hair from digital photos before you post them on dating sites. It appears that this is biblical. According to an article on a website specifically for Christian singles sponsored by eHarmony.com, all women in the Bible "knew the importance of having healthy, beautiful skin."[1]

Women in the Bible understood the importance of healthy skin because Leviticus commands that those with bad skin be kicked out of the neighborhood. It seems that as far as Leviticus goes, righteousness runs only skin deep. The dermatological is theological—despite assurances elsewhere that God looks at the heart instead of on outward appearances (1 Sam. 16:7). Sure, Jesus breaks protocol by reaching out to touch lepers in the Gospels (*leper* being a biblical catchall term for every sort of skin infection), but he does so only to heal them. We never catch Jesus simply hanging out with lepers. There is Simon the Leper, who hosted a party for Jesus (Matt. 26:6; Mark 14:3), but in all likelihood the nickname referred to his former condition. I'm guessing that the party was to celebrate his being healed by Jesus. Had Simon still been a leper, there would have been no party because nobody but Jesus would have come within a mile of Simon's house.

However, Kristi the Leper, who currently suffers from eczema, suggested an analogy between her condition and moral transgression: "If you don't stop it early on, it can spiral out of control." It is true that throughout the Bible, sin and disease are often analogous (Mark 2:9–12). While eczema would not imply moral guilt, its tie to imperfection and decay was enough to bar you from worship and from community life. Committed to our month of obedience, our weekly group dinners therefore meant cordoning off the blemished for the sake of purity. While those with skin problems felt somewhat silly about having to tousle their hair and shield their mouths, the healthy among us were even more uneasy. We felt as if we were all back in high school shunning the kids with acne. Was this what God intended?

Uncomfortable with having the Lord appear adolescent, some Bible versions attempt to mitigate against the Levitical obsession with complexion (and mucus and mildew and shellfish) by relegating the concern to "ceremonial" cleanness, a reference to the now-obsolete tabernacle ritual. (The New International Version goes so far as to insert "ceremonial" as an adjective modifying "cleansing"—Lev. 14:2.) Like sacrificial animals themselves, God's people were expected to present themselves without spot or blemish (ceremonially speaking) in order to enter the tabernacle.

But Leviticus wasn't just concerned about clean skin in worship. The infected weren't barred only from the tabernacle but from polite society itself. This has led others to argue that the epidermal injunctions were simply God's way of managing ancient Israel's public health. Contagious skin infections had been known to wipe out entire populations. In a day without modern medicines, getting infected people out of the camp could keep everybody else healthy. It wouldn't do any good to make the long journey across the desert if nobody was alive once you got to the Promised Land. However, if health was God's main concern, why didn't he just inoculate the nation against infection to begin with?

The Bible says nothing about purity being reserved only for the erstwhile tabernacle, even though it is true that skin infections no longer get you barred from church (though they may get your child barred from the church *nursery*). Moreover, Leviticus does not express any particular concern for ancient health and hygiene, though if you greet your neighbor with an extended hand covered in fungus, you probably will receive only a wave offering in return (Lev. 14:12).

Cleanliness is not only set apart for Leviticus. It shows up throughout the entire Bible. Jesus tells a leper he healed in the Gospels to "go, show yourself to the priest and offer the sacrifices that Moses commanded for your cleansing, as a testimony to them" (Mark 1:44).

The "them" in Mark 1:44 is the Pharisees, who by the time we get to Jesus had turned keeping clean into the sum total of one's keeping righteous before God. Even though God was still in the cleaning business, the cleanliness code had become infected. The Pharisees used it as a lever with which they tried to control access to God. Therefore, the leper's "testimony *to* them" is really an indictment *against* the Pharisees and the ways they had distorted the law and burdened the people with legalities the law was never meant to impose. Jesus sternly warns the ex-leper not to speak to anyone until he gets to Jerusalem, because he wants the ex-leper to get there quickly to testify negatively against the legalistic system that loaded people down with guilt and kept them away from grace.

In Leviticus, cleanliness was never about keeping you out, but ironically, it was about getting you in. As Beena, one of our

Levites-for-a-month, observed, "The priest followed up with the patient on the seventh day. This shows that the patient wasn't isolated just for being unclean or as a punishment."

CLEAN HOUSE

Leviticus never goes so far as to treat the unclean as unworthy, but it does expect cleanliness in practically every aspect of life. In addition to your skin (and the skin of your animals), cleanliness also applies to your clothing, your house, and your diet. Leviticus 11 prohibits eating rats, lizards, skinks, and chameleons, along with numerous other nondelectables. A disappointed Ian remarked (facetiously) how difficult a Levitical diet was going to be to keep: "I can't begin to express how often I crave eels, bats, red kites, geckos, and weasels." However, Leviticus also famously excludes pork (Lev. 11:7), causing Ian (much less facetiously) to express grave consternation over giving up his beloved Slim Jims, which he assumed were filled with all kinds of swine. Thankfully, upon a more thorough examination of its ingredients (as Leviticus required), Ian was relieved to discover that while Slim Jims do contain questionable soy-based additives and all sorts of beef and chicken by-products, raising Levitical concerns about mixing two kinds of meat (Lev. 19:19), there was no pork.

While walking home one evening, Lisa stumbled upon a group of protesters marching against a meeting of something called the Pork Council. (I'm not making this up.) Like any good investigative Levite, she pulled out her trusty video camera and queried the protesters as to why they thought that Leviticus prohibited eating pigs. One protester (grateful to learn this Levitical tidbit) fashioned how he thought "it had something to do with the fact that pigs don't have sweat glands and they have to wallow in mud." I guess that would make swine unclean.

Not only is Leviticus fastidious about the food it prohibits, but it is also meticulous about how to prepare the food it allows. Brian took a trip to a kosher butcher shop to check out the prescribed meatpacking process. Beef and bird butchery entailed the removal of entrails, fat, and all the blood, after which the meat was then dipped into water and salt to remove any remaining trace of blood. A rabbi came in every day to oversee the entire process. Assuming that the butcher had also been reading Leviticus, Brian asked him why they went to all the trouble. The butcher told Brian that studies have shown that indigestion can be avoided through kosher eating. Brian asked whether there were spiritual advantages to eating kosher (wanting to give the butcher another chance). The butcher replied that he hoped when he died he would get into heaven because he had kept his meat so clean. He also admitted he didn't really think about heaven much. Actually, Leviticus doesn't mention heaven either, but since the tabernacle was designed according to heavenly specs, I guess you could draw a connection. Brian scored one for the butcher.

If you read the earlier chapters of Leviticus on sacrifice, you are struck with how the process for preparing sacrificial beef sounds so much like the kosher preparation of pot roast. The reason is that the same meat Leviticus considered fit to eat was the same meat it considered fit to sacrifice. Remember, the sacrificial meat that atoned was the same meat that nourished. This still doesn't explain why pork was verboten. Nothing makes for better eatin' than a fat pig roasted over fire! Paul and Brandy both confessed to pork cravings during the Levitical month. After the month was over, Paul uploaded a Facebook video showing his delight at eating bacon again (including the grease that coated his lips). Brandy did the same with a scrumptious spiced hot dog.

Keeping kosher during the month presented its problems beyond the pork-related cravings it created. Paul went at it with his wife over the contents of a certain sausage he refused to eat even though she insisted it was turkey (bacon deprivation kept him in a bad mood). Paul wondered, "How could I be sure she knew all the ingredients? Nobody knows all the stuff that goes into sausage!"

This raised the question of why any creature God created would be regarded as unclean and unfit to eat or sacrifice. Some suggest that the limits on permissible meat are God's way of limiting the innocent slaughter of animals. Adam and Eve were ostensibly vegetarians prior to biting the notorious forbidden fruit. It's not until they sinned that an animal was killed (Gen. 3:21), and that was not yet for food. God conducted the first animal sacrifice for Adam and Eve in order to make skins to cover their nakedness (nakedness being indicative of their shame). Moreover, hunted animals are not kosher in Leviticus, which therefore prohibits any killing for sport. And since kosher animals are mostly herbivorous, the sacrificial process makes a statement against predation too. The point seems to be that cleanliness incorporates the high value God places on life, except, that is, on the life of the clean sacrificial animal. (Being labeled "unclean" therefore has at least one advantage.)

Others argue that cuisine is a good way to distinguish between groups of people. As a Southerner living in New England, I never felt at home as long as there was no good fried chicken. Likewise, Jews in New England stay away from the lobster (which in my opinion would make summer in New England very difficult). Since God was concerned that his people be *peculiar*, a distinctive menu made sense. People have to eat every day; what better way to remind them of their peculiar identity than with their food? This was Thomas's experience. He wrote,

> In normal non-Levitical life, we peculiar Christian folk hope that we appear different in some way. Not superior or better, or

standing outside sporting events inside sandwich boards giving out anti-hell propaganda, but just different. Maybe displaying a quiet peace and comfort and assurance about the future that makes people wonder, "What's with him? I fancy some of that." In abnormal Levitical life, not eating pork has made standing out pretty easy. And while it took a bit of explaining, good and deep conversations have been made possible by the impossibility of bacon.

Whatever the reason an animal was deemed unclean, eating a pig or a skink (a shiny lizard) made you unclean too. In fact, simply touch a skink (or at least a dead skink—Lev. 11:31) and you'd be as unclean as if you'd eaten it. Andrew noted that much of this aspect of Levitical living is left to personal integrity. How would a priest know if you'd touched a lizard? You would have to police yourself. It's like golf, in which there's no referee to call a penalty: the expectation is that you respect the game and your fellow players enough to call penalties on yourself when you break the rules. The expectation in Leviticus is that you love God and your neighbor enough to play by the rules of God. Of course, even without referees, as Andrew reminded us earlier, one should be motivated by the fact that God is always watching (which probably applies to golf too).

GOING SEPARATE WAYS

Kristen read the rest of Leviticus's agricultural laws as respectful to creation and therefore to the Creator, which could be read as another aspect of keeping covenant. "In my mind," she wrote, "factory farming does not mesh with respecting creation. So no more supermarket meat counter products for me. I'll only eat meats from animals that were humanely and naturally raised (e.g., cows are made to eat grass, not corn). I expect this will mean I'm eating a lot less meat."

Kristen got caught at a dinner meeting where

unsurprisingly, it did not occur to my amazingly organized meeting coordinator to provide a Levitically sanctioned meal, much less my "meat is only acceptable if it comes from tree-hugger hippie chickens (or cows or sheep) who spent their animal lives holding hands and skipping around a pasture" approach to Torah. Usually there's some sort of vegetarian something so I didn't think to give her a heads-up, but not this time. Uh-oh. Now what? These meetings are *long*—I didn't want to wait until I got home to eat. Moreover, as I was someone's guest, I needed to be graceful more than Levitical, so I grabbed a chicken burrito. Chicken is a clean animal; there's no blood. It would have to do.

Upon further reflection, with a full tummy, this was a mistake. Leviticus makes no provisions for "Do this unless it's awkward or uncomfortable or seems somehow rude." If these prohibitions just don't work with the way you live your life, change the way you live your life. Come out and be ye separate. So if waiting until I got home wasn't a good option, I should have run across the street and gotten something meatless to eat—even though that would have left our amazingly competent meeting organizer, who did absolutely nothing wrong here, feeling awkward and uncomfortable. That should not be my concern.

But here's my problem. I really didn't want to do that. And while my tree-hugger hippie approach to eating meat does have a moral dimension, a lot of these prohibitions do not—they're being separate largely for the sake of being separate. As my consultant told me the other day [throughout the

Levitical month Kristen employed assistance from a couple of Jewish friends she labeled her "consultants"], being a "holy nation" is not the same as being a "righteous nation." Israel is supposed to be both, but they're not the same concept, and most of Leviticus is far more about holiness.

While Kristen is correct that righteousness and holiness are not the same, they are more closely related than one might think. Righteousness addresses justness and blamelessness—that is, being right with God. Holiness addresses distinctiveness and devotion. Part of Israel's distinctiveness (holiness) was that they were right with God, made so by God. The challenge, as with holiness, was staying right with God. (This is where having to sacrifice all those animals came in.) Thus there can be no holiness without righteousness. And while it is true that Leviticus only mentions righteousness in the context of just courts and just scales (19:15, 36), it is presumed as part of the basis on which the sacrificial system necessarily operated.

Kristen did get this:

I have no trouble standing out from the pack when it comes to righteousness (theoretically—I make no bold claims about my actual track record on the subject). I want my lifestyle to look different. I want to handle money differently. I want to treat people as ends rather than means. I want to recognize myself as God's beloved creation, and when I know that, then chasing after status and acclaim seems pretty ridiculous. If I live that way, I'll look plenty different. But all of that is about righteousness, which is a different question. Separation for separation's sake continues to grate.

Kristen's post drew a number of comments. Simon agreed:

The Torah never makes allowances such as "If this rule makes your host uncomfortable, you may elect to skip it." Here is where Levitical living is hard: if you had several of us with you, and all of us agreed that we would not eat meat no matter what the cost might be (or maybe if I am the one running across the street to buy the Levites some veggies), then it would be easier to live out that rule. Sure, we would be weird—but then we would be weird *together.* There is some strength in numbers, after all.

Mary Frances liked Simon's take: "The community aspect of 'living Levitically' in the time of the Israelites often gets overlooked."

Brandy pushed back on the difference between holiness and righteousness. Kristen replied that "some things are forbidden because they're bad things to do. Don't lie, don't steal, don't murder, don't abuse the poor or the aged. That's righteousness. Other things are bad things to do because they're forbidden. Don't eat from unclean animals, don't work on the Sabbath.... That's holiness. My consultants do not think bacon is inherently evil—it's just forbidden for them."

Again, any distinction between holiness and righteousness is a distinction without a real difference. Kristen's delineation between righteousness as the counterpart to immorality and holiness as the counterpart to disloyalty shows this. Murder and lying are sins because each violates the nature of God, who is the source of life and truth. Sacrificing or eating animals deemed unclean and working on the Sabbath are forbidden because they violate the nature of God, who is pure and holy. Unrighteousness and unholiness are both failures of faith in God. In addition, unrighteousness and unholiness are both failures to love your neighbor. To murder or lie does explicit harm to another. To break kosher or break Sabbath disrupts the community. Holiness is not about separation for separation's sake but for the sake of a community devoted to God. Yet such separation does not mean reclusiveness. It's not separation *from* the world (isolation) but separation *for* God (devotion) that matters.

ON YOUR MARK, GET SET, WASH

As for cleanness, it is not as closely related to holiness as is righteousness. A holy person is a clean person, but being clean is not the same thing as being holy. Cleanness or purity operated as more of a starting point for holiness. That God chose Israel to be his people made them clean by virtue of their being God's choice. God chose them because he loved them, not because they were special or deserved it. You see the same thing in the New Testament. Jesus says to his disciples, "You did not choose me, but I chose you" (John 15:16); "You are already clean because of the word I have spoken to you" (John 15:3). In Christian practice, baptism symbolizes this reality. Baptism, inasmuch as it is the initiation rite of the church, represents one's starting point on the journey of faith. The waters (by faith) wash you clean before God. The trick is *staying* clean.

This was the case in Leviticus. Holiness was the goal, and cleanness was the starting point. You had to keep clean to get to holy. Plenty of people profess faith, but not everyone who professes faith keeps faith. Just as baptism is no guarantee of obedience, being clean was no guarantee you kept clean—which is why God made the guidelines for cleanness specific and behaviorally oriented. What you believe is not as much what you *say* you believe as what you do. Somehow, strict attention to diet, hygiene, and health contributed to the spiritual health of ancient Israel. They were headed for the Promised Land, a land flowing with milk and honey but also a land oozing with degenerate (yet enticing) Canaanite culture. Staying clean would require staying away from those aspects of Canaanite culture that would sully their souls.

Growing up, I always thought it silly how the kids from fundamentalist families never got to go to the movies. Their parents didn't want aberrant Hollywood values seeping into their children's heads. While the rest of us kids piled into theaters on Friday and Saturday, the fundy kids had to practice piano or play outside (which helps explain why my fundy friends are great musicians and athletes while I excel at managing my Netflix queue). Back then I rolled my eyes at fundamentalist parents' puritanical logic, but now as I watch movies I'm often bothered by the gory violence, the obscene sexuality, the abusive language, the drugs and deceit—and that's just the PG-rated stuff. Only I never get up and leave the theater or eject the DVD. No, just as I did as a youngster, I sit there and soak it all in, too often amused by the very things that disturb me. And while no movie has yet caused me to do drugs, cheat on my wife, blow away my enemies, or careen my car through city streets, surely I've been desensitized to these things. My soul has been sullied.

God rightly worried that his chosen people would choose to go with the perverse Canaanite flow, threatening both their own integrity and their witness as his people on earth. Thus more than merely clean, God called his people to be holy—set apart, peculiar, uncommon, special, and distinct. God's people were not to "conform any longer to the pattern of this world, but be transformed" (Rom. 12:2) into a countercultural community of righteousness and love. Cleanness may have been their starting point, but holiness was their goal and their ultimate identity. They were to be like God (Lev. 11:44). Yet because cleanness and holiness went together, uncleanness jeopardized everything. This is why God made such a big deal about staying clean.

MR. CLEAN

In addition to eating right and eradicating skin infections, Leviticus 13 and 14 devote verse upon verse to eradicating mildew from a variety of fabrics and from all sorts of surfaces for the sake of cleanness. Clean skin and clean food aren't sufficient; what you wear and where you abide matter too.

This led Andrew to conduct a thorough search of his apartment for mildew. He located extensive infestation on his bathroom tile and ceiling, which he diligently (and digitally) documented with his video recorder—much to his wife's consternation. In Leviticus, if your house had spreading mildew that couldn't be removed after scraping and replastering, you had to tear down your house and haul it out of town—just as you had to do with yourself if you had a spreading infection. Interestingly, the word translated "mildew" in Leviticus is the same Hebrew word as that for "infectious skin disease" (ṣāra'at). They are both considered "afflictions." Mildew and skin infection are the same thing (Levitically speaking), because they come from the same source. Leviticus 14:34 names God as the source of contamination! Some attribute affliction to God's judgment, while others attribute it to God as Creator (all nature comes from God, including mildew and bacteria). If nothing else, that mildew comes from God does help explain why the stuff is so hard to remove.

For Walter, the problem was plaster dust. While managing to get rid of all his mildew, he was left with a film of dust that managed to make its way into every corner of his house. Whenever he and his wife thought they'd cleaned it all out, more dust would emerge. Though plaster dust is kosher, its residual effects weren't so different from the mildew it replaced. Walter wrote,

Sin is like plaster dust. It gets everywhere, into every nook and cranny of the house of my soul. It also never gives up. Two weeks after the contractor left, we're still cleaning and sneezing from all the dust. The dust keeps coming and coming. It is the monotony of having to clean every day that is such a pointed reminder that holiness, like dusting, is a task that needs to be taken up each day.

Like Walter, Mary Frances recognized an analogy between uncleanness and sin, though her analogy for sin was household clutter. She performed an "overhaul" cleaning on her tiny apartment—makeshift tabernacle included—scrubbing every surface and floor. Afterward, she admitted a great deal of pride in her tidy home. "It's very exciting to look into a laundry basket and find that it is totally empty (cheap thrills, I know)." But less than twenty-four hours later, she (somehow) was astonished to find the clutter creeping back into place ("as if there was any question as to who had tarnished my clean little kingdom"). She was reminded that there is always a need to clean up our lives, inside and out. Sin constantly lurks, looking for any crevice to invade.

Of course, Levitically speaking, the only problem with these analogies is that unlike mildew and fungus, sin (whether as plaster dust or household clutter) decidedly does *not* come from God. Cleanliness is next to holiness, but it is not holiness itself. Likewise, uncleanness is next to sinfulness, but it is not a sin. Nor is being clean the same thing as being forgiven (though cleanness can be an *outcome* of forgiveness). More than anything, cleanness goes to motive. Psalm 24 asks, "Who shall ascend the hill of the LORD? And who shall stand in his holy place?" Answer: "He who has clean hands and a pure heart, who does not lift up his soul to what is false and does not swear deceitfully" (vv. 3–4 ESV). Sin generally begins with a desire to sin (or at least an openness to it).

Purity of heart counters that desire. It's all about motivation and intent.

"Clean hands" had to do with a clear conscience, though clearly, washing the dirt off your fingers or the mildew from your shower did little to purge your soul. However, the ritual did remind you of the need to get your heart right before God—just as the habit of saying grace reminds you to be grateful to God even if you don't always feel grateful when you say it. It may seem perfunctory at times (and even embarrassing if you're with somebody who prays out loud in restaurants), but remembering to be thankful may occasionally be worth a little public humiliation. Going through the motions can clean up your motives. My brother Greg tells the story of his high school daughter and a young suitor who came by to pick her up for a date. Greg has definite rules for dating his daughter, which include *how* you pick her up for a date. The young man picking up my niece on this particular night pulled up to their house. But rather than getting out of his car and coming to the door, he summoned her by laying on his car horn. My niece grabbed her stuff and was on her way out when Greg stopped her, telling her in no uncertain terms that any boy who wanted to date *his* daughter had best respect her and her father by coming to the door and introducing himself. After blowing the horn a couple more times, the boy got impatient and called my niece on her cell phone and told her to hurry up. *Bad move.* My brother got on the phone and let the young suitor have it. Needless to say, that boy and my niece never went on *that* date. It's not that Greg minded his daughter going out with this boy; it's just that he wanted him to demonstrate the good intentions of his affections by showing some respect—the kind of regard that signals you think of somebody as more than just a pretty face.

It's the same with God. "Clean hands and pure heart" show proper respect and good intentions. Yet there are so many things that mar our intentions and render us unable and unwilling to want God rightly. Everybody on the Leviticus project stumbled over constant obstacles to keeping clean and moving toward holiness. As Ophera bemoaned, "This is too hard." There are simply too many other things vying for our attention—unclean things that we, frankly, prefer. Thankfully, God does not give up on us. Knowing that holiness is best for us yet unwilling to coerce us into it, his only option is to show us how much we need it so that we'll want it bad enough to do something about it. How does God do this? *Affliction.* Skin infection. If there's one thing we cannot ignore, it's our skin. I think God used skin infection as an object lesson to teach us to want holiness.

Now whether you interpret skin infection as a random act of bacterial nature or God's judgment is not the issue in Leviticus. The object lesson was not the infection itself, but what happened once you got it. God declared the infection unclean and ruled that you were to be quarantined from the community and from the tabernacle. You stayed outside the camp until you healed, however long that took. Of course just as Leviticus attributed the infection to God, so the Bible attributes all healing to God, however healing happens. This is what made Jesus' healing those lepers so significant. Not only did the healing identify Jesus as God the Healer, it also identified him as God the Cleaner.

WHATEVER IT TAKES

Having your skin infection healed was not the end of the story. Had health and hygiene been the lesson, you'd have been let back into camp as soon as you were no longer contagious. But that's not how it worked. In Leviticus, once your skin cleared, you still had to come up with the following: A priest. Two clean, wild birds. Some cedarwood. A piece of crimson yarn. Hyssop.

Fresh water. A clay pot. Soap to wash your clothes and body. A razor to shave yourself. Three lambs without blemish. Six quarts of choice flour and a cup of olive oil. During my reality sermon series on Leviticus, I paraded all these elements into church for effect (though I had to settle for a photograph of the two wild birds and three lambs without blemish). It took me a couple of days just to get everything together (not to mention many minutes of explanation to merchants along the way—"You need crimson yarn for *what*?"—because Leviticus 19:11 doesn't allow you to lie).

Each of these items had a specific purpose. The priest served as the intermediary between you and God. God did the healing; the priest checked to verify whether you had healed (the priest was not a doctor). Once healed, the priest killed one of the birds and then dipped the live bird into the blood of the first bird (all mixed with the water and the cedar and the yarn and the hyssop in the clay pot). He then took the hyssop and sprinkled you with the mixture before releasing the live bird back into the wild. The reason the bird was wild was so that it wouldn't come back. It was sort of like a scapegoat with wings (Lev. 16), transporting your uncleanness far out of reach. The cedar and the yarn, both colored red, further symbolized blood as life and atonement. Cedar, as the building material for houses, and yarn, as the material for clothing, also underscored the importance of a clean house and clean clothes (remember, infection is infection wherever it lands). The fresh water was literally "living water," and the clay pot represented your own frail, jar-of-clay self (which explains the apostle Paul's use of the metaphor to describe the cleansing power of Christ inside his humble self: "We have this treasure in jars of clay to show that this all-surpassing power is from God and not from us"—2 Cor. 4:7). The hyssop plant worked like a sponge, soaking up the life and washing you with it, reminiscent of King David's prayer of confession in Psalm 51: "Cleanse me with hyssop, and I will be clean" (v. 7).

You would do all of this, but you still wouldn't be done. After the birds and the blood and the hyssop and the jars, you still had to wash your clothes, shave and bathe, and then wait seven days, an echo of creation itself. It took seven days to create the world (six to make, one to rest). It would take at least that to create you anew. Only then could you come back into camp, but there was still no getting near God until another seven days passed. On the *second* seventh day, you washed and shaved off all your hair, which made you look clean as a newborn baby (born again, anyone?). On the eighth day, a day in the Bible that always signals heaven and new creation, you finally entered the tent and offered your reparation offering of lamb, flour, and oil (an appropriate Levitical meal). The whole ritual indicated the massive and glorious movement from uncleanness, sin, and death to life, new birth, and a new start. You moved from the realm of impurity outside the camp to first being restored to your community, and then to being reunited with God. You got clean and then you got holy. It's a trajectory that the book of Hebrews picks up on in chapter 12: "Make every effort to live in peace with all [people] and to be holy; without holiness no one will see the Lord" (v. 14).

Now I trust you're a little overwhelmed by all this. None of the Levites-for-a-month even attempted to pull all of this together (catching one wild bird, let alone two, is *very* difficult). We were all left thinking, *Who in their right mind would ever go through all of that?* Then again, when you're infected with sores and cut off from your friends and your God, who *wouldn't* do whatever it took to get well and make things right again? You would want that with all of your heart. You would crave with the purest, most focused desire the very thing that was best for you. You'd want it so badly that no obstacle could get in your way—no matter if it took spools and spools of yarn and a whole cord of cedar, you'd want to get clean and holy. Maybe this explains why God put all those requirements in there. Not only to make you badly want all your relationships restored, but also to make it so you'd not want to be unclean again. Perhaps this is also why he causes or allows affliction to begin with. It's certainly why God eventually allowed *himself* to be afflicted in Christ (Isa. 53:7). He desperately wanted a restored relationship with his people. And he desperately wanted for them to be as devoted to him as he was to them. He wanted them (and us) to be holy as he is holy.

Lisa reluctantly acknowledged she understood why God might go to such extremes to get to her.

This whole issue of cleanliness has been a real struggle this month and I have wanted to reject it because it just didn't make sense, but now I'm beginning to get it. If I, as an unrepentant, pernicious, afflicted sinner who was set apart, was then consequently made aware of my uncleanness and finally found my affliction healed, I couldn't just run back into camp and start sitting in the same seats as everyone else, eating from the same dishes, giving handshakes and hugs all around. I had to go through that whole reentry process.

I won't go through all of that process unless I have felt the pain of separation, the ugliness of my sin, my need for community and for God, and the desire to truly be pure and clean again. That yearning for being in right relationship will sustain me through the ordeal of getting through the process of becoming touchable again. It's a purity you only really understand when you know what being unclean means. How it impacts your relationships to others and how you are perceived by others, how you are cut off from them and from God. How it makes you see your ugliness and the consequently deep desire to be truly rid of it.

How then would we embrace purity? How different

would my heart be in seeking God? I might be willing to do anything. I might actually give up my sins and not see anything alluring in them whatsoever. I might actually become truly repentant.

Too often I settle for good intentions instead of right intentions. My sins are not made apparent to me in the way that God sees them and I certainly don't acknowledge the effect they may have on others. I put on this cloak of grace without ever seeking the kind of cure that removes them instead of just covering them up.

Unfortunately for the Israelites, they never really learned this lesson. Instead, they confused the ritual with reality, thinking that by going through the motions they could control their own righteousness. The prophets tried to set them straight. Micah asked,

> With what shall I come before the Lord
>> and bow down before the exalted God?...
> Will the Lord be pleased with thousands of rams,
>> with ten thousand rivers of oil?...
> He has showed you, O man, what is good.
>> And what does the Lord require of you?
> To act justly and to love mercy
>> and to walk humbly with your God. (Micah 6:6–8)

Similarly, Jesus chastised the Pharisees who refused to heed the prophets' correction. "You hypocrites!" he said. "You clean the outside of the cup and dish, but inside they are full of greed and self-indulgence" (Matt. 23:25). Paul (one of our Levites-for-a-month) described growing up in one of those fundamentalist families where he wasn't allowed to go to the movies. However, he was allowed to watch disallowed movies at home on his VCR.

All that mattered, it seemed, was how you looked to others. Just keep that cup and dish clean.

Purity of heart—*cleanness* of heart—is all about motivation and intent. Integrity demands that the heart match the hands (Ps. 24:3–4). What you believe is what you do. But precisely because of what we *really* believe, we try to fake it with our actions. This is why Leviticus is necessary. By getting at our skin, God gets under our skin and exposes us for the fakes and the failures we are.

But in the end that's just what we need. When you see yourself as you are, covered with sores and living life on the outs, all you want is to get clean and get right with God, whatever it takes. That's purity of heart. And as Jesus said, "Blessed are the pure in heart, for they will see God" (Matt. 5:8).

Chapter Five

Does Getting Worked Up About the Sabbath Count as Work?

There are six days when you may work, but the seventh day is a
Sabbath of rest, a day of sacred assembly. You are not to do any work;
wherever you live, it is a Sabbath to the LORD.
       —Leviticus 23:3

Read the New Testament (or at least the Gospels), and you'll find that nothing causes greater consternation than Sabbath keeping. In each Gospel, among Jesus' greatest offenses in the eyes of his nemeses, the Pharisees, is the way he flouts the law regarding the seventh day. The fourth commandment is clear: "Remember the Sabbath day by keeping it holy. Six days you shall labor and do all your work, but the seventh day is a Sabbath to the LORD your God. On it you shall not do any work" (Exod. 20:8–10). Yet Jesus heals (Matt. 12:13), allows his disciples to pick grain (Mark 2:23–24), and instructs a formerly paralyzed man to carry his mat (Mark 2:11; John 5:8)—all in violation of strict Sabbath code. In the book of Numbers they stoned a man for merely carrying wood on the Sabbath (15:32–36).

Such severity about the Sabbath carried over into my Bible Belt childhood. For anyone growing up in the South, keeping the Sabbath holy was a civic as well as a religious responsibility. Sunday was set apart (kept holy) from the other days of the week. Stores were closed. Nobody but firemen, policemen, and ministers (ironically) worked. If your car broke down, too bad. You shouldn't have been driving in the first place. You were supposed to be resting or in church. (Okay, so we had to drive to get to church, but once there I always slept.) God himself worked for six days and rested on the seventh. Who are we to do any differently?

These days, even in the Bible Belt, Sundays are as busy as any other day—and that's not just at church. Stores are open, as are plenty of mechanics' shops. Add to that kids' soccer games, chores that need attending to, and assignments that need completing in time for Monday. As stressful as this is, for some of my friends it's better than the stress they experienced under what they felt to be the dismal weight of Sunday obedience. Many kids bailed on Christianity altogether once they finally made it to college. I remember one friend in particular telling me that he'd stopped going to church because for the first time in his life he wanted to experience something on Sunday besides guilt.

What happened to mutate a day designed for rest and worship into such an onerous burden? You could blame the Pharisees. Over the centuries, Jewish rabbis labored to define in pedantic detail what "keeping holy" and "not working" precisely meant. In so doing, their interpretation of the law stiffened into strictures more rigid than the law ever intended. Their rules forbade sowing, plowing, binding, threshing, winnowing, grinding, sifting, baking, shearing, stirring, washing, beating, dyeing fabric, carrying anything, making a loop, starting a fire, stopping a fire, weaving or separating two threads, opening a book, riding in a boat, tearing paper, writing or erasing, tying a knot, picking the bones out of a fish, or combing your hair. The prohibition against carrying anything on the Sabbath fueled the Pharisees' indignation against

Jesus for healing that paralyzed man (Mark 2:11; John 5:8). So absurd was their concern for Sabbath breaking (by both Jesus and the man who picked up his mat and walked) that they totally missed the miracle. In the end it was the Pharisees who suffered true paralysis.

NO REST FOR THE WEARY

We Levites-for-a-month weren't interested in becoming Pharisees-for-even-a-day. But we still publicly wrestled with what it meant to "keep Sabbath" (can you eat out or not, watch play-off football or not?). Unexpectedly, readers of our Facebook chronicle erupted with Sabbath input. From Jews in Israel to fundamentalist Christians in Idaho, concern over what to do with the Sabbath (and exactly on what day of the week to do it) made keeping the rest of Leviticus seem simple. When it came to the day of rest, there was no rest.

Jesus had tried to clear things up by saying, "The Sabbath was made for man, not man for the Sabbath" (Mark 2:27), but as with most sayings of Jesus, we were left uncertain as to application. Could we cook lunch or mow the yard? The only way forward was to try keeping some serious Sabbath, since that is what Leviticus instructs. So Lisa, Brandy, and Kristi worked themselves silly on Saturday in order to chill on Sunday. Granted, working so hard in preparation for Sabbath made rest a lot easier, since they were totally exhausted come Sunday. Nevertheless, they agreed that their Sabbath rest was fabulous and posted numerous smiling faces on Facebook to prove it. Still, they looked pretty tired when we saw them in church that night. Wasn't there a way to step into this weekly rhythm without getting wiped out by it? Some of the Jewish folks we encountered admitted that it takes a lot of practice. Holiness always does.

Thomas acknowledged that for him, "as a boy, Sundays were, if you'll pardon the pun, observed religiously in my home. There was no work or schoolwork done, no television watched, and no sport played. Furthermore, to avoid responsibility for making other people work, my family didn't go to shops or restaurants either." While insisting that these Sabbath restrictions were not excessive ("Looking back, I see vast value in having Sunday stand so distinct from every other day—rather than just church before laundry and errands"), his attempts to return to Sabbath keeping as part of the Levitical month met with dubious results. "I started out not buying things, not eating out, and not even driving. But then I began ferreting for ways to push the envelope—like having other people buy things for me or order 'too much food' and then share with me, and I, being holy, could hardly spit in the face of such honest hospitality."

Having created the world in six days, God rested on the seventh and commanded that his people do likewise. The Lord rested not because he was tired and needed a nap or because work was a bad thing. God's rest reflected his satisfaction with the goodness of his work, his enjoyment over a job well done. Sabbath celebrates completion, fulfillment, and satisfaction. The prohibition of work was not a denigration of labor, but a reminder that work is not all there is to life.

The Sabbath, while generally applied to the seventh day, is not solely confined to it. The Day of Atonement (Lev. 16:29), which falls on the tenth day of the seventh month, is also called a Sabbath. The Feasts of Pentecost and Tabernacles (Lev. 23), both holy weeklong festivals, emphasize the eighth day as a Sabbath. The precise day was not at issue as much as precise behavior—namely, "You are not to do any work" (Lev. 23:3). To work is to participate in God's creativity; to rest is to enjoy creativity's fruits. To keep Sabbath was to stick your toe into eternity and enjoy a taste of heaven itself. "There remains, then, a Sabbath-rest for the people of God," the book of Hebrews declares. "For anyone who enters God's rest also rests from his own work, just as God did from his" (4:9–10).

ETERNITY TAKES FOREVER

As the Lord of the Sabbath (Matt. 12:8; Luke 6:5), Jesus declared himself the source of that Sabbath rest: "Come to me, all you who are weary and burdened, and I will give you rest.... For my yoke is easy and my burden is light" (Matt. 11:28, 30). If Jesus' coming inaugurated the ultimate rest toward which Sabbath pointed, in a very real sense we're already there. While the early Christians (all of whom were Jewish) still kept Sabbath (Saturday), they added to it the Day of Resurrection (Sunday, making for the first weekend!). Theologically speaking, that the resurrection occurred the day after Sabbath (the seventh day) meant that it happened on the all-important eighth day, the first day of eternity. The Lord's Day on the first day of the week, Sunday, became for all Christians symbolic of the first day of new creation. In time, as the church became increasingly composed of Gentiles, Sabbath was folded into the Lord's Day as Christians set aside time to worship and break the bread of Communion in anticipation of that communion of rest they would one day enjoy every day with Christ and one another forever.

Whether you call it Sabbath or the Lord's Day, this day of weekly sacred time celebrates a job well done while providing a time-out from the aggravation and disappointment of earthly toil. Freed from the worries of this world, weekly worship expands our horizons to encompass the horizons of heaven. At the core of Christianity's creeds is the conviction that in Christ, what is coming far exceeds what now exists, even in its most glorious renderings. By reminding us that this life is not all that there is, Sabbath whets our appetite for eternity. At least that's the idea.

We Levites approached Levitical Sabbath keeping with this view toward eternity but found the experience not yet in line with the reality. Anticipating eternity is tougher than you'd think. Kristen wrote about doing all the work that doing no work on the Sabbath required: "I suppose I could have been really on the ball and gotten all my 'general life' stuff done during the week, but I'm not that on top of things. I'm in trouble. I'm to rest on the Sabbath day, not some day that works best for me."

Lisa provided a glimpse of the hard work of resting in a video she produced titled "Lisa Has No Nightlife." Observant Jews throughout history set aside a day prior to the Sabbath to get ready to rest. The Gospels refer to it as "Preparation Day" (Mark 15:42). Rather than being out on the town dancing with her friends, Lisa stayed home to cook and clean in preparation for the Sabbath, since no cooking or cleaning would be allowed the next day. She also had a big project due at her job on Monday that she would not be able to work on come Sabbath, so she had to finish that too. As a "last-minute kind of girl," Lisa admitted that Preparation Day mostly just left her stressed. Good thing she took the next day off.

For serious Sabbath keepers, getting ready each week becomes routine. But that doesn't make Preparation Day any less work. Sokol had a Jewish friend invite him to a full-blown orthodox *Shabbat*. He described the *Shabbat* meal he ate with his friend's family as akin to the Thanksgiving feast he eats once a year. For this particular *Shabbat,* all the cooking had happened on Thursday night, since his hosts still had to go to work before sundown Friday (Jewish *Shabbat* runs from Friday sundown to Saturday sundown). Jewish Sabbath rules prohibit lighting or extinguishing light once *Shabbat* commences. For Sokol's friend, that meant turning on all the lights that needed to be on for the twenty-four hours (living room, bathroom, ceremonial lamps) and turning off the lights that needed to be off (bedroom). Sokol proudly added, "I was glad to see that my reading of Talmud-related books came in handy when I reminded them that the refrigerator light needs to be turned off during Shabbat." Otherwise, whenever they opened and closed the refrigerator (allowed), the light would come on and go off (prohibited). I'm sure his friends were glad for Sokol's reading as they irksomely unscrewed their refrigerator bulb. The religious rationale (though not in Leviticus) has something to do with "creating and destroying light," a big Sabbath no-no. God let there be light on Day One, and to create light yourself imitates God's creativity. But since God rested from creating light on the seventh day, you're not to mess with the lights either.

The notion that we rightly imitate God in our work and rest was why the New Testament Pharisees became so furious with Jesus for *wrongly* imitating God by working on the Sabbath. It wasn't that the Pharisees thought that God *literally* rested on the Sabbath. After all, if God actually stopped working, all of nature, providence, and life itself would stop working too. God would have to create the heavens and earth anew every week. Did this make God a Sabbath breaker? Of course not. As Maker of heaven and earth and Author of the law, God was allowed to work on the Sabbath—albeit God and God only. This helps make sense of the Pharisees' getting so incensed over Jesus' working on the Sabbath. For a *human* to work on the Sabbath was more than disobediently refusing to rest; it represented a deliberate grab for a piece of divine prerogative. To work on the Sabbath meant you considered yourself to be on par with God. By working on the Sabbath, Jesus insinuated that he was the Son of God, and thus heir to divine power. And then by declaring himself "Lord of the Sabbath" (Matt. 12:8; Mark 2:28; Luke 6:5), he removed any ambiguity. Concluding Jesus to be a blasphemer of the highest order, the Pharisees had no option but to plot for a way to kill him (Mark 3:6). Nobody can claim to be like God and live (Lev. 24:16; John 19:7).

Before Sokol could partake of the *Shabbat* feast, there was a *Shabbat* worship service to attend. The synagogue service was fairly straightforward—filled with psalms and prayers ("but no women," he noted). Inspired by the worship and later stuffed full by the food, Sokol determined to rest for the rest of his Sabbath, which at this point still had twenty hours left to go. He began by walking home from the synagogue instead of driving (which was not only obedient but necessary, since he needed to walk off his dinner). But that only took him thirty minutes. With nineteen and a half hours left, he started to get a little nervous. Would he be able to pull this off? He went to bed early (knocking out eight hours), but Saturday loomed. Having decided no e-mail or TV (e-mail is work, and TV is TV), he had time to read Leviticus some more when he woke up. But then the doorbell rang and his four-year-old daughter's new dollhouse arrived in the mail. How was he not going to put it together for her when she'd been pining for it for weeks? (His daughter was not living Levitically.) Chalking it up to doing good on the Sabbath (Jesus said that was always al-lowed—Matt. 12:12), he helped her construct the dollhouse. The problem was that now he was in work mode, with eight hours of Sabbath remaining. He started getting restless (pun intended) and stayed that way for the rest of the day (pun intended again). Lisa was right. Rest can be very stressful.

MODERN-DAY LEGALISM

Stressful also described all the discussion Sabbath keeping gen-erated. During the Levitical month, no other topic created so much stir (even though much stirring is considered work). Readers of the Facebook site (Jewish, Christian, and Jewish-Christian) who weighed in on proper Sabbath observance were most disturbed by what they considered to be our blatant disregard for celebrating Sabbath on the actual Sabbath (Saturday rather than Sunday). A reader from Massachusetts vehemently insisted that humans were not at liberty to shift the days of God's calendar. A reader from Israel concurred. He argued that to move the Sabbath to Sunday was an open door to sin, since you'd now be working on the real Sabbath (Saturday) and resting on the wrong one. A reader from London added that Christians who observed Sunday as Sabbath were severing themselves from the chosen people of Israel by not observing the Jewish Sabbath. Another reader from Missouri noted that while it was interesting to read about Christians voluntarily keeping something approaching the Sabbath, keeping Leviticus for just a month sadly presumed that Leviticus doesn't really have any application for Christians. The only way to abide it (endure it?) was to reinterpret it. Build a silly tabernacle in your apartment and call that obedience. And on and on it went.

Brandy couldn't help but push back against the whole specific-day-of-the-week commotion:

> While there is a command from the Lord to designate the seventh day of your week as a Sabbath of rest to the Lord, there is absolutely no biblical requirement to have that Sabbath only fall on a Saturday. The Bible says that there are six days when you can work, but you need to refrain from work on the seventh one. I don't see anything that says, "Oh, and that week should start on day X." In short, while for many years I have failed to honor the Lord by keeping the Sabbath, my failure wasn't in that I didn't keep it on Saturday; it was that I never kept a seventh day of rest, *period*.

Like Sokol, Brandy and Lisa did attend *Shabbat* service on a Saturday (although theirs was with a Messianic Jewish—aka Christian—congregation rather than in a Jewish synagogue). Under a post titled "Ladies for Leviticus Meet Jews for Jesus," Brandy wrote,

> It was so much fun! People are very welcoming, and it was a neat experience to see this blend of Jewish tradition and Christian faith, but in a way that was very accessible to two Gentile first-timers. We shared about our experiment, and folks were very interested in hearing what is afoot. Additionally, three bold subjects allowed themselves to be interviewed on camera. I came out feeling very joyful from the worship and the message, as well as super energized about how this experiment is going to change my life and relationship with God.

No word on whether the experience persuaded Brandy to do Sabbath on Saturdays.

Nevertheless, Andrew felt compelled to ask the obvious: "Should Christians keep a Sabbath at all? Or is it a command (and a good one) for Jewish people only?"

Theologically speaking, the main difference between Jews and Christians when it comes to Sabbath (aside from the day) is the Sabbath's ultimate aim. For Jews, Sabbath aims backward at the creation account and Torah. God made the earth in six days and rested, and thus God commands we honor his creation by abiding by this cycle of work and rest. For the Christian, Sabbath aims forward toward the new creation and Jesus as the personal embodiment of what Sabbath portends (Matt. 11:28).

You find parallels to this effect in the Gospels. For instance, God created humans in his image and gave them the tree of life on the sixth day in Genesis (2:9). On the sixth day in the Gospels,

God, having become human himself in Christ (John 1:14; Col. 1:15), hung on the deadly tree of life to redeem the sins Adam introduced in Genesis. On the sixth day, God completed his creation work and called it good (Gen. 1:31). In the Gospels, Jesus completed his redemptive work and declared, "It is finished" (John 19:30) on the sixth day (with Easter proving how good it was). God rested from his work on the seventh day in Genesis and in the Gospels (with Jesus R.I.P. in the tomb). And then, "early on the first day of the week, while it was still dark," the women arrived at the tomb to discover Jesus back at work (John 20:1). New creation had begun (as creation itself had begun on the first day of the week). New creation is not something left to the sweet by-and-by, but an eternity already started with the resurrection. This is how the apostle Paul could write to the Corinthians, "If anyone is in Christ, he is [now!] a new creation; the old has gone, the new has come!" (2 Cor. 5:17).

Some theologians argue that the fourth commandment no longer applies since it has been fulfilled in Christ (Matt. 5:17). This is supported, it seems, by Paul's own dismissal of "Sabbath day" as a "shadow" rather than the "reality" who is Christ (Col. 2:16–17). Yet these same theologians rarely will say that the other nine commandments no longer apply. Murder and adultery are still wrong, as are misusing God's name and dishonoring your parents. This leads other theologians to insist that the fourth commandment applies as much as it ever did. Though the early church kept the Sabbath and the Lord's Day distinct (since they were still working out their own Jewish-Gentile differences as Christians), by the fourth century as Gentiles became the majority, the church lost the Sabbath *day* but kept the Sabbath practices by applying the fourth commandment to the Lord's Day. (This practice also was influenced by the Roman emperor Constantine's declaring the venerable day of the sun—Sunday—to be the venerable day of the Son in AD 321.)

This Sabbath application occurred even though the Lord's Day wasn't technically the seventh day, but the day after. Again, this is significant. While the resurrection (and new creation) occurred on the first day of the week (like original creation) theologically speaking, it can also be said to have occurred on the *eighth day*, which in Leviticus and the remainder of the Bible is always a marker for heaven and the end of earthly time (since earthly time is marked in seven-day increments). The year of Jubilee, the fiftieth year (Lev. 25), and the Feast of Pentecost, the fiftieth day after Passover (Lev. 23), are both "eighth day" events. (Jubilee occurs the year after seven seven-year periods and Pentecost the week after seven seven-week periods.) They are also both Sabbath events, meaning no work. Likewise, the Lord's Day, whether you view it as the seventh day, the first day, or the eighth day, remains a Sabbath day to be kept by Christians, even if all we do is keep feeling guilty about it.

Simon finally managed to squeeze in a proper Sabbath at the end of the Levitical month. However, he wasn't able to squeeze in a Preparation Day (the first sign of trouble), which meant he had to get up and get to a pile of dirty dishes in the sink before he could rest guilt-free. "What to do next?" Simon asked himself (which is a really bad Sabbath question—the second sign of trouble). As a computer professional, Simon finds tinkering with computer gears in his spare time to be pretty relaxing, so he decided to add a little memory to a firewall device since it seemed to be running too tight most of the time. In order to add memory to his firewall, he first had to adjust the existing hard disk partitions to reflect the newly added memory. So he put the new memory in and got a backup copy of the firewall on a CD, and then realized that he had no idea how to work the partition utility (I hope you're following all of this). Next, he resized the partitions using another tool. But then he noticed that the firewall had stopped recognizing one of its network cards. "It was as if someone had unplugged the card from the system while it was turned on. Actually, that was exactly what the status message said, 'Unplugged.' Not good." He rebooted the firewall and hoped that would solve the problem, but the entire machine froze. *Definitely* not good, since this symptom strongly suggested hardware failure.

What had started as a simple memory installation turned into an all-hands-on-deck rescue operation of his computer. "This had moved way past relaxing." Simon was in the realm of serious concern. Time to take a walk. He bundled up his kids, and he and his wife went for a brisk stroll—determined to enjoy some Sabbath even if there were merely three hours left. Yet all he could do was think about his computer, which was now in pieces with parts strewn all over his bedroom floor.

Back from his walk, he spent the next two hours attempting to rectify the problem to no avail. By sundown, "I was sweaty, tired, angry, hungry, thirsty, and in absolutely no mood to celebrate whatever remained of the Sabbath" (which was now beside the point, since there was nothing left). That night he sat down to read Leviticus 26 (Simon was reading a chapter a day and it was the twenty-sixth day of the month). The second verse smacked him in the head: "Observe my Sabbaths and have reverence for my sanctuary. I am the LORD."

Simon wrote, "I let out a bitter laugh and then thought about how my day would have been had I taken the Sabbath more seriously and placed it on a higher priority. I let my 'hobby' turn me away from the Lord and my family, and what an awful experience that was." Of course, if he continued to read, I imagine verse 21 punched him in the hard drive: "If you remain hostile toward me and refuse to listen to me, I will multiply your afflictions seven times over, as your sins deserve." That might explain the computer crash. Ouch.

As a harbinger of heaven, Sabbath calls a halt to the hopelessness of human striving and to the frustrating limits of this finite world. Sabbath draws attention away from worry and stress, expanding your horizons to encompass the horizons of heaven. Sabbath frees you from the aggravations and disappointments of your deadening, earthly labor by stopping you and pointing you toward the delightful satisfactions that can accompany work done well—delight experienced by God himself in his raising Christ from the dead. By reminding us that this life is not all that there is, the Lord's Day draws us into eternity. It sets our hopes on what shall be. While the Levites who tried to take Sabbath seriously struggled to do so, I think they would say they struggled because they had never taken it so seriously before (except for Thomas, because his parents forced him). Part of the problem is that we have a hard time equating joy with obedience. Sure, the idea of rest as *vacation* sounds awesome, but rest as vocation? It's not something many of us are very good at.

SUNDAY LUNCH

While I failed at setting aside any serious Sabbath (Levitically speaking), I do remember one Sunday years ago that for me epitomized what a true Christian Sabbath experience on earth can look like.[1] I had the occasion to join the Reverend Peter Gomes for lunch one Sunday after worship at his church, the Memorial Church in Harvard Yard. I was invited because a friend, David Fisher, was preaching at Memorial Church that morning. During the worship service, the hymns and the anthem, as well as the liturgy and prayers, reverberated God's glory. And David's sermon proclaimed God's goodness in Christ for the whole campus to hear. (Understandably, the administration of Harvard is not always pleased with such goings-on in the center of their secular campus, despite its Christian origins.)

Following the worship service, Reverend Gomes escorted David and me, along with other guests, to his house for Sunday lunch. "It is my assertion," Reverend Gomes intoned as we took our seats around his sumptuously decorated table, "that the primary rehearsal for the glories of heaven's wedding banquet cannot be enjoyed over cocktails, at a Saturday picnic, nor at the fanciest of dinner parties. No, in order to fully rehearse what awaits us at the banquet table of God, the only suitable candidate is Sunday lunch. Having feasted upon the Word of God in worship, we now feast with great thanksgiving upon the provisions of God set before us at this table."

And what a feast it was: carrot soup with coriander and fresh dill, braised pork tenderloin with cranberry mustard glaze, puree of butternut squash and basmati rice—all served with a lovely 1997 Apulian Copertino Reserva. (Reverend Gomes is privileged to enjoy the services of a professional cook—one of the several perks of his position at Harvard.)

After partaking of this delicious spread, as we enjoyed our mixed-berry shortcake with orange blossom cream and a merry theological repartee, Reverend Gomes rose from his chair and reiterated how, while he was growing up, his mother, no matter their weekly difficulty at making ends meet, would always set aside their hardship and worries for Sunday lunch. Moreover, it was mandatory that their Sunday table include guests—most of whom were friends but some of whom were people they had met at church for the first time. And if nobody was available from church, his mother saw to it that they picked up somebody on the way home ("When an alien lives with you in your land, do not mistreat him.... Love him as yourself"—Lev. 19:33–34). Reverend Gomes continues this practice; one of our lunch guests was collected as we walked over from church.

Among the guests who previously had graced the table at

which I sat was the late, renowned chef Julia Child. Of course, having Julia Child at your table would generate no small amount of anxiety (another reason to be blessed with a professional cook—let him be anxious). I imagine it was rare for Julia Child to be invited to anyone's house where she wasn't the one doing the cooking. "Julia," Reverend Gomes had said to her, stating the obvious, "it must be terribly difficult coming to others' homes for lunch, knowing their awareness of your scrutiny over what's on their table."

"Oh, Peter," Julia Child replied, "it's never *what's* on the table that matters, but *who's* on the chairs!"

With this as his cue, Reverend Gomes commenced to go around the table and lavish praise upon each of his guests. Modesty prohibits me from repeating what he had to say about me. Suffice it to remember that praise is seldom so magnanimous as when lauded upon someone you've known for less than an hour. But isn't such praise indicative of God's grace too? We're never surprised that our idealized estimations of others recede as we get to know them better. Familiarity still breeds contempt. But with God, who knows us better than we could ever know ourselves, familiarity breeds grace. And such unwarranted grace does indeed raise you up and give you the best seat in the house (Eph. 2:6). It instills you with gladness.

I couldn't help but smile. Having enjoyed the worship and Word of God, the wonder of hospitality and the honor of being a guest, I left that house that Sunday feeling just the way I think I was supposed to feel. I felt rested. I felt full. I felt glad. I felt happy. I felt good. And if that was just a small part of what heaven will be like, I felt excited for it. *That* was a Sabbath. Now if only I could have figured out how to get invited every Sunday.

Chapter Six

Loving Your Neighbor with an Unshaven Face

Do not hate your brother in your heart. Rebuke your neighbor frankly so you will not share in his guilt. Do not seek revenge or bear a grudge against one of your people, but love your neighbor as yourself. I am the LORD.

—Leviticus 19:17–18

As we've seen, Leviticus 19:18 famously commands, "Love your neighbor as yourself." Jesus said that as long as you love God, keeping Leviticus 19:18 automatically keeps everything else. Maybe obeying the Bible isn't so hard after all! But then that lawyer in Luke's Gospel (wanting to justify himself) made the mistake of asking Jesus to define "neighbor" (Luke 10:29). Jesus responded with the story of the good Samaritan, and suddenly what looked so simple became exponentially difficult (self-justification does that).

While the Levitical month led to a lot of picking and choosing over which commandments to keep and which to ignore (as if this was unusual when it comes to the Bible), the New Testament's emphasis on Leviticus 19:18 made heeding this command inescapable. Some of the commandments (such as "Do not mate different kinds of animals"—Lev. 19:19) could be kept passively, since none of us had animals to mate. But given the example of the good Samaritan, "Love your neighbor as yourself" would require definitive action.

Most people know Jesus' story: "A man was going down from Jerusalem to Jericho, and he fell among robbers..." (Luke 10:30 RSV). Personally, I dislike this story because it makes me feel guilty for not being like the good Samaritan. I hear Jesus describe the religious people who passed by the needy man and think, *I do that*.

Jesus then rubs salt in my guilt by having the hero be a despised enemy of the robbed and beaten man as well as of the religious folks who steered clear of him. This Samaritan took pity on an injured man he was supposed to hate and helped him above and beyond what anybody would have been expected to do. Given centuries of animosity between Samaritans and Jews, we would not have been shocked had the Samaritan steered clear too. Imagine a member of Hamas coming upon a wounded Israeli by the road, or vice versa. Or in America, imagine an African-American coming upon an injured white supremacist. Frankly, we would not have been shocked had the Samaritan stopped and given the Jewish man a swift kick in the ribs for all the racist torment piled on Samaritans by Jews over the centuries.

Instead, not only does the Samaritan interrupt his travel schedule, risk infection by patching up the Jewish man's bloody wounds, use up his own costly oil and wine as salves, surrender the comfort of his own burro, and search for an inn, but he also gives the Jewish innkeeper permission to run a tab to cover whatever expenses the beaten man's convalescence might incur. Who does that? And what happens when the Jewish man wakes up and discovers he's been cared for by a Samaritan? What does Mrs. Samaritan say when she sees her husband's Samaritan Express credit card bill? The impracticality and the irrationality of the Samaritan's actions should have earned him the title of "the *stupid* Samaritan."

It's interesting to note that in telling his story, Jesus never answers the lawyer's question. The lawyer asked, "Who is my neighbor?" Jesus answered, "Who acted like a neighbor to the man who fell among robbers?" (Luke 10:36). By centering his reply on the loving acts of a Samaritan (whom faithful Jews would have considered a heretic), Jesus underscored the fact that "loving your neighbor" is not about defining the object (neighbor), but about doing the verb (love). Taken literally, to "love your neighbor" is to love the person *nearby* (which is why the Samaritan stopped when he happened upon the robbery victim). Certain that Jesus (or Leviticus) did not intend for me to wait until I happened upon someone beaten and robbed, I decided to go with the literal definition of neighbor—the people who live nearby.

Living in a city where my neighbors are mostly (and deliberately) unfamiliar, keeping Leviticus 19:18 required some effort. Northeastern urban protocol generally precludes much of my deeply instilled Southern hospitality. Act overly friendly in my 'hood, and my neighbors are likely to tell me to go do anatomically impossible things to myself. I tried to befriend my upstairs neighbor, since we share a two-family house, but she seems too freaked out by my being a minister. She refers to herself as "the pagan" in my presence and generally tends to pass me by on the other side, perhaps for fear I'll try to convert her or something. (Actually this was okay for the Levitical month. Leviticus forbids contact with pagans—or at least their practices [20:23]).

So this left me with my neighbors who reside on either side. On the right side lives an elderly woman I've never met (and only seen once). I was shoveling my sidewalk after a snowfall and noticed that her walk wasn't cleared, so what better way to love my neighbor than to shovel her walk too? So I did (and in doing so also scored one of several gold stars for Leviticus 19:32, which commands respect for the aged). On the left side lives a couple who just had twins. We've said hello over the fence in the summer, but that hardly counts for love, so I decided to take over a baby gift.

I knocked on our next-door neighbor's door, and the understandably harried mother answered. Covered in baby food and plainly annoyed at the interruption (her babies screaming in the background), she looked at me suspiciously, having no idea who I was. I introduced myself and offered her the gift, which only made her more suspicious. Nevertheless, she took the gift and summarily slammed the door, leaving me to wonder whether this was how the Samaritan got treated once the robbed guy he helped healed from his wounds. Whatever. Leviticus never said that your neighbors had to love you back. And even if they do, Jesus said, what's so great about that? Even tax collectors and pagans love those who return the love (Matt. 5:46–47). So rather than feeling slighted, I decided to thank God for allowing me to go the extra mile (Matt. 5:41).

Now I could have stopped there, feeling all righteous and obedient as I did, except that at two in the morning, after my wife and I had wrestled our four-month-old daughter to sleep and settled down for our own long winter's nap, the upstairs party girl embarked on an earsplitting splurge of some seemingly pagan revelry. We didn't know exactly *what* she was doing, but whatever it was, I swear she was going to come crashing through the ceiling onto our heads. Aggravated and angry, I threw on my clothes, stomped up the stairs, and banged on her door, demanding, "What the heck is going on up here? It's two in the morning!" My neighbor looked at me wild-eyed, grunted, and then slammed the door in my face. However, she must have comprehended something because the wild ruckus ceased.

Later, remembering the commandment, I felt bad for yelling at my neighbor. But then I read Leviticus 19:17: "Rebuke your neighbor frankly so you will not share in [her] guilt." By telling pagan party girl to pipe down, I was being obedient to God and didn't even know it! Good ol' Leviticus.

Verses 17 and 18 in Leviticus 19 work together as a couplet. Each phrase of verse 17 corresponds to a parallel phrase in verse 18. Thus, "Do not hate your brother in your heart" in verse 17 corresponds with "Do not seek revenge or bear a grudge against one of your people" in verse 18. "Rebuke your neighbor frankly" in verse 17 goes with "Love your neighbor as yourself" in verse 18. And "[Do] not share in [her] guilt" in verse 17 corresponds with "I am the LORD" in verse 18. The first phrasal pair presents the prohibition: "Do not hate; do not bear a grudge; do not seek revenge." The second pair presents the positive alternative, "Rebuke frankly and love." The final pair gives the reason for doing the positive alternative: "Otherwise you'll be guilty because God said so."

For you visual learners, it looks something like this:

Leviticus 19:17	Leviticus 19:18
Prohibition	
"Do not hate your brother in your heart."	"Do not seek revenge or bear a grudge against one of your people."
Alternative	
"Rebuke your neighbor frankly."	"Love your neighbor as yourself."
Reason for the Alternative	
"[Do] not share in [her] guilt."	"I am the LORD."

So by telling the party girl to pipe down, not only was I being obedient to God, but I was *loving* my neighbor too. The only problem was that I *hated* her the whole time I was doing it. To love may include bringing grievances into the light, but only if the goal is not humiliating the person with whom you are aggrieved. The purpose of a loving rebuke is forgiveness and reconciliation. But few people rebuke with forgiveness and reconciliation in mind. We rebuke because we're angry. Retribution, not reconciliation, is on our minds.

Perhaps this is why Jesus brings the matter up again in the Sermon on the Mount: "You have heard that it was said, 'Love your neighbor and hate your enemy,'" Jesus preached, referring to Leviticus 19 (Matt. 5:43). Except that nowhere in Leviticus 19 does it say "Hate your enemy." It does say *"Do not hate* your brother" (Lev. 19:17, emphasis added). Apparently the commandment got twisted around over the centuries to mean that as long as you don't hate your brother, it's okay to hate your enemy. Moreover, if you do hate your brother, you can just label him your enemy and that'll make hating your brother okay too. It's the old Torah two-step. Bearing a grudge became obeying the law. But Jesus rectified *that* dance step by making it clear that loving your neighbor included loving your enemies too. It's what made the despised Samaritan the *good* Samaritan.

But what if your rebuke isn't received as the love you intend? What if your neighbor scorns your forgiveness or refuses reconciliation? What then? Again, Jesus answered that question by asking: "If you love those who love you, what reward will you get? Are not even the tax collectors doing that? And if you greet only your brothers, what are you doing more than others? Do not even pagans do that?" Instead, Jesus says, "be perfect, therefore, as your heavenly Father is perfect" (Matt. 5:46–48). This was Jesus' reiteration of Leviticus 19:2: "Be holy because I, the LORD your God, am holy."

Yet because such holiness remains impossibly hard (nobody's perfect), the tendency is to do our own version of the Torah two-step, the most popular being to treat God's commands as idealistic. We'll claim that the Bible sets the bar too high on purpose in order to force us to cry uncle and concede our need for Jesus. While appropriate, it is also convenient. By leaving the bar so high and labeling the hard commands idealistic, we leave any actual obedience out of reach. That way we're not really to blame.

But I don't think that Jesus intended "Love your neighbor as yourself" and "Love your enemies" to be treated as idealistic. Likewise, I don't think that God, when he told the Israelites in Leviticus 19:16 not to spread slander, meant "It's okay to slander as long as you think the slander is true or the gossip is especially juicy." And when God told them to leave the gleanings of their vineyards for the poor (Lev. 19:9), he didn't command it with the qualification, "Unless you're still hungry." The same with Jesus. He didn't say, "Love your enemies, unless you're mad at them." He said simply, "Love your enemies." Loving your enemies is not idealistic. You can do that. It's difficult, but it's not idealistic.

This is where grace comes in. The grace that forgives us our sins against God is what makes it possible for us to forgive others' sins against us. It's hard, but by grace we can do it. And when we fail to do it, there's grace to prod us to try again. This reality prompted Kristi to post this piece from Catholic mystic Thomas Merton:

> It is not complicated to lead the spiritual life. But it is difficult. We are blind, and subject to a thousand illusions. We must expect making mistakes almost all the time. We must be content to fall repeatedly and to begin again to try to deny ourselves, for the love of God. It is when we are disappointed at our own mistakes that we tend most of all to deny ourselves for the love of ourselves. We want to shake off the hateful thing that has humbled us. In our rush to escape the humiliation of our own mistakes, we run headfirst into the opposite error, seeking

comfort and compensation. And so we spend our lives running back and forth from one attachment to another. If that is all our self-denial amounts to, our mistakes will never help us. The thing to do when you have made a mistake is not to give up doing what you were doing and start something altogether new, but to start over again with the thing you began badly and try, for the love of God, to do it well.[1]

Because loving your neighbor was never meant to be idealistic, Leviticus 19 lays out specific detail as to what it looks like. Of course, right after the command to love your neighbor comes the weird prohibition against wearing clothing woven from two kinds of material (Lev. 19:19). What does this have to do with loving anybody? Thomas hoped to find out by eschewing blended fabrics for the month and wearing only linen trousers. Unfortunately, all that Thomas learned was that linen is a bad choice in cold weather. Others tried to figure out why Leviticus 19 also adds the prohibition against shaving your face (v. 27). Or not eating leftovers (v. 6). Frankly, the entire chapter reads like a bunch of leftovers tossed together into an odd Levitical casserole.

However, there is some logic to the oddness—and it all still relates to loving your neighbor. As a preacher, allow me to alliterate. Chapter 19 can be broken into four connected parts; I'll call them *covenant, community, Canaan,* and *compassion.*

COVENANT

The *covenant* section, Leviticus 19:1–8, focuses on covenant loyalty. The covenant is the arranged marriage between God and his people (via Moses) at Mount Sinai (in the book of Exodus, chapters 19 and following). Basically the Lord says, "I'll be your God. You be my people. I'll take care of you. You be holy like me." Any mention of Mount Sinai naturally begs mention of the Ten Commandments (Exod. 20:1–17), and sure enough, all ten are reiterated in Leviticus 19: worship no other gods or idols (v. 4), honor your parents (v. 3), keep the Sabbath (vv. 3, 30), make no useless oaths (v. 12), no stealing (vv. 11, 13), no hating (aka murder, v. 17), and no coveting (v. 13), sexual immorality (v. 20), or lying (v. 11). To be loyal *to* the covenant is to live *by* the covenant, which is a big reason why you love your neighbor.

Admittedly, verses 5–8 do seem to go off on a tangent about fellowship or peace offerings, but this is actually a practical illustration of what keeping covenant looks like. The meat of the peace offering was the only sacrificial meat that laypeople were allowed to eat (the priests ate the other offerings except for the burnt offering, which was totally burnt). Taking the sacred sacrifice from God's house to your house for dinner was sort of like bringing holiness home. And not just home, but to your neighborhood (loving your neighbor implies loving the neighborhood). You would share the sacrifice with family, friends, and strangers in what amounted to a peace offering block party. And if you had a pagan party girl in the neighborhood, so much the better. Meals were a way to make peace in ancient cultures. Food still functions that way in modern cultures. Cooking a delicious dinner for somebody is a great way to make amends. The peace offering made peace with God; the sacrifice atoned for the sin, and the leftovers celebrated the forgiveness.

The peace offering was also an expression of thanks. Eating with such purpose reorients your approach to food. Rather than simply eating for sustenance or to alleviate boredom, meals become the means of communal thanksgiving (which is why Thanksgiving is called Thanksgiving). We Levites found that the weekly meals we ate together as a tribe were sort of like Thanksgiving. We prayed and thanked God, and in doing so we reinforced our own sense of community. Levitical obedience is by design a collective enterprise. As such, the meals we shared provided opportunity to share our struggles too. Making peace is not just about ending strife; it is also about creating safety and security. Feeling safe opened us up to one another so that we were able to talk about the lessons and burdens of obedience. Predictably, sharing our burdens lightened our loads—which is exactly the way Leviticus is meant to work.

The rules for eating the peace offering meat were clear: two days, and then toss it out. Why? Because God Almighty said so. Okay, but meat was a luxury and no family could consume that amount of beef in two days (which is why you were commanded to share it). Would it be so bad to put the leftovers in the fridge for later? There is always a tendency to rationalize our disobedience by cloaking it with reasonableness. It's not enough that God would command it. We need to understand his purpose for doing so. And if we can't understand his purpose, then we don't feel obliged to do it. But what if his purpose only became obvious once you did it?

Paul described chowing down on some clam chowder only to realize afterward that he'd broken the Levitical prohibition against shellfish. Paul wrote, "I am failing miserably at the 1 percent of the law written in Leviticus that I'm trying to keep. I can only imagine how bad it would be if I tried to follow everything. I now have a new appreciation for the wrath of God, though clearly this is not the position I would want to be in." Of course, what Paul also had was a new appreciation for the grace of God.

Obedience was no easier for Kristi than it was for Paul (or any of us). This fact was one for which Kristi's own mother could vouch, particularly in regard to Leviticus 19:3 (respect your mother and father). Kristi described writing her mother a note "apologizing for the infinite sea of irreverent deeds and hurtful words I've spoken over the years. One note isn't enough to make amends, but it's a start." Given the difficult nature of keeping covenant and the provision of the peace offering for the sake of a new start, I guess Kristi could have sent her mother a slab of beef. But I don't think she thought of that.

COMMUNITY

Leviticus 19 continues with the topic of food, moving from beef to barley as it picks up the practice of *gleaning*. Verses 9–10 provide a good transition from *covenant* to *community*. While God's covenant applied specifically to the Israelite community, part of that application addressed attitudes toward those outside on the community's margins (again, loving your neighbor). While holiness may have to do with being set *apart*, it has nothing to do with being set *against*. Thus God commanded that when harvesting your field, whatever produce you accidentally dropped was to be left on the ground for the poor and the alien to gather. If your harvesting methods proved too thorough, then you were commanded to be sloppier for the sake of the needy.

Inasmuch as generosity toward others is often (or should be) motivated by gratitude for one's own windfall, gleaning was another way to give thanks to God. But why not just *give* the poor the extra produce? Why make them pick it up for themselves? The reason was that gleaning allowed the unemployed to enjoy the dignity of work. Moreover, gleaning allowed the poor and alien to be recognized as sharers in the fruit of the good land that God had given to everyone. Gleaning also gave the poor access to worship. Throughout Leviticus, God provides discounts to the poor when it comes to sacrifices. For those who couldn't afford an animal to sacrifice, grain offerings could substitute. Gleaning supplied the grain. And if you've read the book of Ruth, then you also know that gleaning was a good way to catch a husband.

While Mary Frances didn't own a farm or a field, she decided to give gleaning a try (though not for the sake of catching a husband). She thought it very cool that God made this provision for the poor.

> I tithe and make regular charitable donations, but I don't have much extra money to give away (at least I don't think I do; God might have a different opinion on the matter). I don't have fields or vineyards either. But I do have a financial harvest that is straight from God. So, for the month, I decided that my "gleanings" would be all the random loose change that accumulates in various corners of my apartment and couch and purse and car and is never put to good use. I set out an empty jar and every few days deposited the loose change into it. I'm proud to announce the grand total came to $20.09. I'm not so proud to admit that the $.09 got lost in the seat of my car, so I just settled on giving away an even $20.

After much mental (and Facebook) debate about whether to donate the money to a worthy charity that works with the poor or just hand it directly to someone who is poor, Mary Frances opted for the latter. Her general policy was to give only to credible organizations that can vouch for how the money is spent. But something struck Mary Frances about the Levitical injunction to simply leave the gleanings for the poor to pick up at will. Much like God's grace, the gleanings were freely given. There were no stipulations on the recipient, no rules commanding that the poor take those extra crops directly to feed their children (versus, say trading them for a box of cigarettes as soon as they were out of sight of the field). "So much of our giving to the poor (and I include myself in this) allows us to write a check and feel good that we have given and done our duty, without having to interact with anyone who is poor. Moreover, our current model of giving is such that we retain control over how and where the money is used. Have we taken some much-needed power and choice away from those we are seeking to help?"

Mary Frances decided to give the twenty-dollar bill to a man she saw begging outside a restaurant near her office.

It was not a remarkable encounter, nothing inspiring to those walking by. As I approached he looked directly at me as he shook his cup and asked for spare change. As I fished around in my pockets for the twenty-dollar bill, we both commented on the weather (very, very cold). As I put the cash in his cup, he said, "God bless you; stay warm," and I said, "You try to stay warm as well. And God bless you too." And that was it.

Like everywhere in Leviticus, the rationale behind gleaning derives from God's own character. (God says "I am the LORD" fifteen times in Leviticus 19, more than in any other single chapter of the entire Bible.) To obey God's commands is to be like God. This is made especially clear in verse 34, where the Lord reminds Israel how he treated them once upon a time: "The alien [or stranger or immigrant] living with you must be treated as one of your native-born. Love him as yourself, for you were aliens in Egypt. I am the LORD your God." In other words, there's an aspect of *identification* that gleaning encourages. To help the poor and alien is to acknowledge that you are no better than they. Better off perhaps, but in God's Levitical economy, that's all the more reason to help.

Kristen brought another new twist to gleaning (like Mary Frances, she also doesn't own a field).

My "harvest," such as it is, comes in the form of a directly deposited paycheck and a portion of that is set aside for the church and other charities. So does that cover the instructions about gleaning? I don't think so. It seems to me that gleaning is about sacrificing some of your own economic efficiency to help people support themselves. Part of the tithe is also set aside for widows and orphans—that's for directly supporting people who cannot support themselves. [Tithing and gleaning are] both important, but they're not the same. The tithe translates relatively easily to a market-based economy. Giving is giving. But what are we to do with these gleaning commands?

Well, a market-based system is better than the alternatives, but we still need to be deliberate about making the system work for people rather than seeing people as cogs in the great machine that is the system. The market is all about efficiency. In commanding his people to allow for gleaning, God tells us that we need to sacrifice some efficiency to enable people to provide for themselves. Which leads me (at long last!) to a point: buying fair-trade products seems to me to be a modern-day equivalent of gleaning. Fair-trade markets are designed to enable artisans in the developing world to support themselves and their families. Consumers pay a premium to buy fairly traded coffees rather than the standard cans of Folgers or Maxwell House, but maybe that's the economic efficiency we're supposed to sacrifice. Maybe accepting that the prices will be somewhat higher is the modern-day equivalent of leaving the gleanings for the poor and alien.

Verses 11–18 move the rest of the way from *covenant* to *community* as the commandments shift from the marginalized to members of the tribe. Many view Leviticus as God's loom for weaving his chosen people into a *choice* people—a tight-knit community of faith, a light-shining witness to other nations. The threads of love and trustworthiness—further characteristics of a holy God—were to be the characteristic fabric of their common life. Lying, cheating, gossip, prejudice, injustice, hatred, vengeance, and abuse—these all threatened to unravel that fabric. Therefore, Leviticus 19 speaks out against them. Yet because simply *not* lying, *not* cheating, *not* gossiping, and the rest might be misinterpreted as *not* doing anything, Leviticus reframes the prohibitions with the positive and active alternative: "Love your neighbor as yourself."

Admittedly the "as yourself" trips up a lot of people. Is God commanding that you love yourself? No. Loving yourself doesn't need a commandment. Most of us do that without being told, if not out of selfishness then at least out of self-preservation. To love yourself *unduly* can be a bad thing, but here Leviticus (and later Jesus, Paul, and James) refers more to the concept of self-concern than self-conceit. Just as you take time for yourself, take interest in yourself, want what's best for yourself, and make excuses for yourself—so you should take time for your neighbor, take interest in your neighbor, want what's best for your neighbor, and cut your neighbor slack. Of course loving others the way you love yourself does not come naturally, and that's without even mentioning Jesus' caveat that you love your enemies too.

Due to the steep degree of difficulty loving your neighbor presents, the lawyer in Luke 10 asked Jesus for clarification and got the story of the good Samaritan.

In Matthew's Gospel, the context is a rich man to whom Jesus suggests that "loving your neighbor as yourself" entails selling his possessions and giving to the poor in order to have treasure in heaven (Matt. 19:21). The rich man famously hesitates because of his wealth, after which Jesus describes how much easier it is to thread a needle with a camel than it is to squeeze a rich man into heaven (Matt. 19:24). Hyperbole notwithstanding, Jesus allows that loving another is formidable. People who make a big deal of the "as yourself" clause (perhaps in an attempt to make loving another easier) imply that the Bible means you're supposed to take care of yourself *first* and *then* you can better love others (since you'll be in a better place to do so, psychologically speaking). But I seriously doubt that Leviticus has psychological well-being in mind. Levitical self-love is nothing more than the self-concern that's part of our biological well-being (not that Leviticus is explicitly into biology). God has wired us to take care of our needs; that's not a bad thing. What's bad (aka *selfish*) is when you *only* take care of yourself. God loves your neighbor just as much as he loves you; therefore, you (like God) must treat your neighbor with the same regard you give yourself.

The New Testament paints a succinct picture of the community this kind of love generates. In Acts 2, we read about all the believers hanging out together and having all their possessions in common. They sold all of their belongings and redistributed the proceeds so that no one lacked what they needed (2:44–45). Unfortunately, redeemed sinners still being sinners, this generous communal life only lasts a few chapters. By the time you get to chapter 5, selfishness has crept back in. And in one of the more disturbing passages in the Bible, God smites a married couple for lying about their own generosity. As a result, we read that "great fear seized the whole church" (5:11). No kidding.

Needless to say, given these consequences, we Levites didn't dare attempt such an intense level of community. Nobody suggested we sell our possessions and share the proceeds with one another (aside from Andrew's suggestion that we all move in together for the month). Nevertheless, even with our erratic obedience, sharing the Levitical adventure spurred deeper concerns for each other's spiritual well-being. It was possible to imagine, if not experience, the kind of community Leviticus and Acts intended.

Sadly, neither the Israelites (with God in their midst), nor the early church (with the Holy Spirit in their midst) could pull it off. Sadder still was that we didn't even try.

I think it's *because* loving others the way you love yourself does not come naturally that Jesus links the command to "Love the Lord your God with all your heart and with all your soul and with all your mind and with all your strength" (Mark 12:30). Loving God makes loving your neighbor possible—or more to the point, God's loving you makes loving him and your neighbor possible. In 1 John 4:19 we read, "We love because he first loved us." To love God back is to be in covenant relationship with God. But if you don't also love your neighbor, then you have no relationship with God since, as John also makes clear, "those who love God must also love one another" (1 John 4:21 TNIV). In this same vein, Jesus said, "Anyone who loves me will obey my teaching" (John 14:23 TNIV). But since obedience does not come without some serious assistance, Jesus added, "My Father will love them, and we will come to them and make our home with them" (TNIV). Loving anybody the way you love yourself does not come naturally, but with Jesus at home in your heart, you have a new nature. Therefore, if you do not love God and your neighbor as yourself, it's not because you *can't*. It's because you're not trying either.

I think we should have tried—even if genuine community can be like threading a needle with a camel. As with sharing your possessions, Jesus did say, "What is impossible for people is possible with God" (Luke 18:27 NLT). I can't help but think that if we had tried, the Leviticus month may have stretched into a lifetime.

CANAAN

Verses 19–31 of Leviticus 19 abruptly shift to mixed seeds, mixed fabrics, and mixed animals. At first you might wonder what in the Sinai desert these commandments had to do with anything else in this chapter. But then you realize that the ancient Israelites were trying to become God's people under pretty godless circumstances. A depraved *Canaanite* culture polluted Israel's Promised Land. *Canaanite* was something of a catchall for a number of idol-worshiping tribes whose posture and practices defied God. Among their worst sins was child sacrifice, but even the lesser stuff was wicked enough that the Lord wanted his people to have nothing to do with them. As with American pop culture that ranks the individual as number one and touts loving yourself as the greatest love of all, Canaanite culture might be seen as promoting a kind of self-absorption even at the cost of your kids. Their religious practices included idol worship and cultic prostitution, which mirror modern America's obsession with power, money, and sex. While each of these can be a means to loving others, when tainted by self-absorption they become barriers to love. Moreover, Canaanite monarchies sought to extend their political power through violent conquest, which ran counter to God's intent for a peaceable kingdom (though admittedly, God commands some pretty hefty violence to get rid of the Canaanites—but that's in Joshua).

As much as such power, money, and sex threaten what it means to live as God's people in our day, so did these obsessions threaten Israel. Thus not mixing fabrics and seeds may have been a practical way of reminding the Israelites not to mix it up with Canaanite pagans and their idols (who mixed up everything). Similarly, Jesus warns against mixing God and power (Mark 12:17) or God and money (Matt. 6:24). The apostle Paul makes a similar point about wrongly mixing God and nonmarital sex (1 Cor. 6:15). You can't sleep around or chase after profit and political power if you're going to follow God.

Not mixing with money was a particular challenge for Levite-for-a-month Paul, an investment manager whose entire occupation was devoted to financial acquisition. As rough as that was, his bigger challenge turned out to be maintaining his wildly growing beard amid the clean-shaven (and ostensibly more greedy) men in his firm. Apparently shaving—and tattoos—were distinctively pagan practices, thus the prohibition against them in verses 27 and 28. Paul was honest with his colleagues about why he decided to forgo his razor, which mostly gave his supervisors another excuse to keep him away from the clients. (They weren't sure about trusting wealth management to someone who's so serious about the Bible, especially since the Bible has little if anything positive to say about accumulating wealth—Luke 12:15–21.) Paul was definitely "set apart," which in all frankness, he didn't like. He complained, "It stinks to be set apart. As a white Caucasian male in America, I was pretty comfortable where I worked. With Leviticus, I really felt out of my element. I think I need to study the Old Testament more if I'm ever going to understand this."

It was a constant struggle to keep the commands that didn't seem to make any sense (even after we tried them out). Obedience for obedience's sake was hardly sufficient motivation. But then again, sometimes there's no other motivation. If the rules are meant to make me holy, but I don't feel like being holy, then at least going through the motions might eventually put me in a holy frame of mind. How many times has going to church when I didn't feel like it turned out to be the right thing to do? (Okay, so as a minister it's my job to go to church; but that still makes my point!)

The good news is that most of the Levitical commands in chapter 19 were quite easy for our group to keep. As far as I know, nobody seduced a slave girl promised to another man (v. 20) or degraded their daughter by making her a prostitute (v. 29). There was, however, a close call with sorcery and telling fortunes, something Leviticus prohibits in verse 26. Sokol ate Chinese one night and was confronted with a fortune cookie ("although it is more a *statement* cookie nowadays"). Even though he admitted it seemed extreme, he passed on the cookie for Levitical reasons. Once again with Leviticus, we were impressed with God's concern for the details of everyday existence.

COMPASSION

Leviticus 19 concludes in verses 32–37 with an assortment of reminders about *compassion*—practicing love and fairness—especially to people who tend to get overlooked. The previous commandment to allow strangers to glean from the fields is expanded to cover generous treatment toward any alien or stranger who chooses to live in your midst. The Israelites were to treat aliens as citizens (v. 34) since they were once aliens themselves in Egypt. Inasmuch as "Egypt" was code for Israel's enslaved past, for us it referred to our own estrangement from God. Without God, we may have been people who discriminated against the immigrant and the stranger for prejudicial and political reasons. But now as God's people, our prejudice and politics must be recalibrated to square with God's impartial and righteous character (Deut. 10:17). "Do not show partiality to the poor or favoritism to the great, but judge your neighbor fairly" (Lev. 19:15).

Having compassion for the poor and the immigrant is a way to revere God, as is rising in the presence of the aged (v. 32). In America, the elderly, like the immigrant, are often relegated to the lower rungs of the societal ladder for reasons that have to do with a lack of reverence. We live in a culture that values youth and novelty over age and experience. Leviticus rejects such misplaced value by commanding respect for our elders. In my house growing up, this meant saying *sir* and *ma'am*. In the city where I live, I give up my seat on the subway for elderly people, something I see few others doing.

Leviticus 19:32 says, "Rise in the presence of the aged, show respect for the elderly and revere your God." I found myself ridiculously (peculiarly?) obeying this command again one Friday afternoon when my wife and I attended the Boston Symphony. Noticing that most of the attendees were elderly, I decided to "rise in the presence of the aged," as Leviticus commands. I stood up, and my wife scrunched down in embarrassment. Fortunately, an elderly woman behind me poked me and told me to please sit down or she was going to call an usher.

The same compassion that applies to the treatment of aliens and aged applies fair treatment to clients and customers too. "Do not use dishonest standards when measuring length, weight or quantity. Use honest scales and honest weights" (19:35–36). For the businesspeople in our tribe, this meant increased diligence in business dealings. Allowing your standards to slip is easy to rationalize when the bottom line is all that matters. But in the Levitical economy, bottom lines are not profit margins. In Leviticus, the bottom line is righteousness and justice, which applies to the customer as well as the seller.

While out grabbing some lunch one day, the cashier gave me fifty cents too much in change. There was a long line waiting behind me as I stood there for a second, wavering. Fifty cents? What does that matter? But then I remembered Leviticus 19: "Do not defraud your neighbor or rob him. . . . Do not use dishonest standards" (vv. 13, 35), and explained to the cashier her mistake. She looked at me dumbstruck, as did the people behind me in line. Fifty cents? She must have said "Thank you" ten times. I left thinking that Leviticus has it right. Holiness permeates everything. And if you can't be faithful in the little things, what chance do you have when it matters?

Chapter Seven

Throwing the First Stone

Do not lie with a man as one lies with a woman; that is detestable.
—Leviticus 18:22

Ask somebody on the street about the book of Leviticus and if they know anything, they likely know about Leviticus 18:22: "You shall not lie with a male as with a woman; it is an abomination" (NRSV). This verse—along with its companion, Romans 1:27—fuels most Christian opposition to homosexuality. To label something an "abomination" is not a sign of approval. In Levitical parlance, an abomination is an offense against God. Verse 22 appears alongside other acts tagged as abominable: Incest. Child sacrifice. Bestiality. Most people would still agree that these acts remain repugnant. Adultery also makes the list—tragic for many, but so common nowadays that most people wouldn't go so far as to call it abominable. This is despite the fact that adultery is the only one of these forbidden acts in Leviticus that cracks the Top Ten (as in Ten Commandments). Making a move on a woman during her monthly period (v. 19) gets mentioned as abominable too, though it's hard to see how. Maybe undesirable and unclean (Levitically speaking), but not abominable.

Brandy wondered if she was the first woman in the group to obediently declare herself unclean for the month (she hoped so, since she was looking for small accomplishments). Yet she also observed,

> It's hard not to get the impression from Leviticus that there's something basically wrong with being female. Somehow women are dirtier. For instance, it takes twice as long to purify oneself after giving birth to a girl (Lev. 12:1–5), and we're of less monetary value too [women were worth thirty shekels to a man's fifty—Lev. 27:1–7]. This chafes, to put it mildly. I'm not being prideful when I assess my abilities in some professional areas as equal to (if not exceeding) most of the men I know who are my similar age with similar experience. Do my girl parts make me less than they? *Whatever*. God treasures me as one of his children, regardless of my price based on the sanctuary shekel.

While it is odd that God puts price tags on people in Leviticus, there's some comfort in knowing that God gave girls a break when it came to the sanctuary shekel. Leviticus 27 addresses making rash promises to God. Rash promises are those promises made to God in desperate moments by even the most hardened skeptics. Believers do it too. You find yourself in an inescapable (kosher) pickle and try to strike a deal: "God, if you are there, then I promise to be a missionary [or its equivalent] if you'll get me out of this mess!" But what if God then gets you out of your mess? You didn't really mean to become a missionary or a priest or to attend church every Sunday. So what about the promise you made to God?

Leviticus allowed you to buy God off. However, the price was not cheap. It cost fifty shekels for men and thirty shekels for women—the prices based on the going rate for indentured slaves.

In effect you were becoming an indentured slave to God, laboring to buy your freedom. One shekel amounted to about a month's pay, so to get out of a rash promise to God cost you three to five years' salary. The lesson? Don't make rash promises to God (Eccl. 5:4–5). As Jesus said, it's better to just "let your 'Yes' be 'Yes,' and your 'No,' 'No'; anything beyond this comes from the evil one" (Matt. 5:37).

As to the abominableness of a woman's monthly period, Leviticus does not assert that menstruation itself was abominable any more than ejaculation was abominable. Leviticus 15:16–18 declares semen "unclean," but not abominable. Why unclean? Maybe it had to do with the discharge of life-giving fluid. Or more specifically, a discharge of life-giving fluid that missed its mark. How did this conflict with the purity of the Lord? As per usual, Leviticus doesn't say. What Leviticus does say is that it was an abomination for a man to have sex with a woman during her time of the month (18:19). Why an abomination? In chapter 20, it says that the man "has made naked her fountain" (v. 18 ESV); or as the New International Version puts it, "He has exposed the source of her flow." Why was this bad? Because the flow was blood. Any contact with blood was forbidden and rendered you unclean due to the connection of blood to life and atonement (Lev. 17). But here the contact is intentional and even egregious. Despite earlier commands against associating with menstrual blood (12:4; 15:19), the couple copulate anyway. Adding abuse to the bloody abomination may have been the man's forcing sex when he knew it was forbidden (18:19). The Israelites were not to be like pagan Egyptians and Canaanites who had no scruples when it came to men getting what they wanted from their women. God demanded that women be treated better than that. Living a holy life meant no going with the flow. "All these [abominations] were done by the people who lived in the land before you, and the land became defiled. And if you defile the land, it will vomit you out" (Lev. 18:27–28). The things that sickened God made the land he made sick too.

BUT WHAT ABOUT HOMOSEXUALITY?

Like sex with a menstruating woman, homosexuality warrants a second mention in Leviticus 20. Alongside incest, child sacrifice, bestiality, and adultery, homosexuality gets listed as an act punishable by death. Though, as Thomas reminded our group, "The fundamental of faith that gets completely missed in blood pressure–raising debates about homosexuality is that the church makes an enormous distinction between its views on a practice and its feelings toward the practitioner." I agree that the Bible allows for a distinction between homosexual *orientation* and homosexual *practice*. It's the same sort of distinction as that between *temptation* and *sin*. To be tempted to do something God forbids is not the same thing as doing it. Even Jesus was tempted "in every way, just as we are—yet was without sin" (Heb. 4:15; see also Luke 4:1–13).

During the Levitical month, I visited an "open and affirming" church (meaning a church that is open to and affirming of homosexual orientation *and* practice). I asked the minister whether he'd ever preached a sermon series from Leviticus. He hemmed and hawed a bit (which may have had something to do with the video camera I had pointed in his face), but then he admitted that he saw Leviticus as mostly an Old Testament anachronism that served to get the Israelites through the desert in good enough shape to make it into the Promised Land. It offered little by way of any practical application now, though it did have the potential to cause harm.

Lisa feared that her gay friends would shudder at any mention of her participation in the Levitical month, knowing that it had everything to do with those two condemnatory verses (Lev. 18:22 and Rom. 1:27). She posted her reservations on a Facebook note, eliciting a response from a gay man who wrote about struggling with his own faith due to the ways other Christians mistreated him for being gay. He said that many of his gay friends had completely abandoned any belief they'd had in God for the same reason. This led to an assortment of other problems, addictions, and emotional troubles. He needed to know why it was so important for Christian believers to obsess over *Jewish* laws that many Jews themselves no longer heed and from which Jesus supposedly released us. Ergo the rub: Are the sexual taboos in Leviticus 18 and 20 culturally particular or universally applicable? Do they apply only to those erstwhile forty years in the desert or to every year since then too?

Given the heat that discussing homosexuality often generates in churches, it is no surprise that we as a tribe spent a great deal of time hashing through it. On the one hand, we wanted to refrain from the overwrought condemnation heaped on homosexuals by many Christians. "Love your neighbor" was not intended for your straight neighbors only. On the other hand, we couldn't take lightly the prohibition writ large in Leviticus. You can't appeal to "love your neighbor" (Lev. 19:18) but then discount the injunction against homosexuality (Lev. 18:22). Can you? There are clear instances where divine commands are relegated to a specific time and circumstance. Commandments to Levitical priests to wear sacred linen garments (16:32) no longer apply, since there no longer exist Levitical priests or sacred garments. There are still sisters, so the commandment against sleeping with your sister holds. And men still grow hair. Does that mean that shaving remains taboo? Plenty of Orthodox Jews say yes. On what biblical basis would you prohibit incest and not shaving?

Many will argue that the safe way to determine the universally applicable is to run Leviticus through a New Testament filter. Jesus said, "Love your neighbor," so keep that. Jesus never said, "Don't shave," so feel free to lather up. Except that Jesus also never said, "Don't sleep with your sister." You see the problem. To be safer, maybe it's best to obey everything in Leviticus that the New Testament doesn't specifically overrule. The apostle Peter asserted, "Just as he who called you is holy, so be holy in *all you do*; for it is written [in Leviticus]: 'Be holy, because I am holy'" (1 Pet. 1:15–16, emphasis added). Overwhelmed by this, most Christians will read 1 Peter and automatically cue up "Amazing Grace." After all, if twenty of us couldn't keep to Leviticus for one month, what chance does anybody have of keeping it constantly? Not much—which is why grace is so amazing.

Still, just because Jesus readily forgives our failures, that doesn't mean we should strive to give him ample opportunity to do so. As the apostle Paul rhetorically asked, "Shall we go on sinning so that grace may increase? By no means!" (Rom. 6:1–2). Salvation may have no requirements (aside from a desperate need for it), but it does carry ethical obligations. This is the purpose of the law. It guides the people God saved by grace into living a life worthy of their salvation. God mercifully delivered his people out of Egypt and told them to "be holy because I am holy." He then gave them the law to show them how. And when they failed, the sacrifices supplied the grace (atonement) they needed so that they could try again.

ADAM AND EVE

When it comes to homosexuality, it may be helpful to go back to the very beginning. From the moment God saw that it was not good for man to be alone and brought Eve onto the scene, sex has been a part of what it means to be made in the image of God. Sex unites a man and a woman together as one, mirroring the interrelatedness and intimacy of the Trinity. As such, sex is holy; its power is designated for the marital promises it both evokes and keeps. Marriage and sex together are so holy that they are employed as the metaphor for the relationship between God and his people (Isa. 54:5; Jer. 3:14), as well as for the union between Christ and his church (Eph. 5:25; Rev. 21:2). Through marital sex, people made in God's image participate not only in God's intimacy but in his creativity too. Love, loyalty, fidelity, joy, and children—these are the things marital sex was made for. It is a holy thing. And since God called his people to holiness, that meant being holy about sex.

Thus God speaks in Leviticus 18: "You must not do as they do in Egypt, where you used to live, and you must not do as they do in the land of Canaan, where I am bringing you. Do not follow their practices" (v. 3). Egypt represented the Israelites' enslaved past. Canaan represented their tempted future. As the Canaanites were soon to be heaved from the land the Israelites would conquer, so would the Israelites likewise be "vomited out" (Lev. 18:28) if they indulged in a lifestyle abominable to the holy God. Of course, for God to ban any behavior all but guaranteed that the Israelites would soon be diving right in. The more perverse Canaanite culture proved to be (and this was before cable and the Internet), the more Israel tolerated and assimilated it. And so just as God promised, the land puked them out. The language in chapter 18 could not be more condemnatory. No wonder people—gay and straight—are so offended by it.

And no wonder well-meaning interpreters work so hard to work around it. Some suggest that the ban only applies to gay sex that occurs in the context of pagan temple worship. Others argue that Leviticus only prohibits sex between two men in a bed belonging to a woman. Some Jewish commentators limit the prohibition against homosexual practice to ancient Israelites since they were the only ones God was talking to. And because there's no direct mention of lesbians, sex between women must have been allowed.

Yet in all of the Levitical talk against interfamily sex, there's no mention of father-daughter incest either, though everyone agrees *that* wasn't permitted. Similarly with limiting the audience to ancient Israel—surely God did not consider incest and child sacrifice okay for everybody else.

AN EQUAL OPPORTUNITY OFFENDER

The most troubling aspect is that homosexuality warrants the *death* penalty. Even if it is an abomination, homosexuality is not as bad as rape or murder, is it? But read on in Leviticus 20, and you'll see that God levies the death penalty against adultery and dishonoring your parents too (both Top Ten sins). There's enough in Leviticus to offend everybody.

It is interesting to note that while there were undoubtedly countless episodes of capital sin among God's people then as now, Leviticus mentions the death penalty being executed only twice: once by God directly and once by the community on God's directive. In chapter 10, two priests (Moses' nephews no less) "offered unauthorized fire before the LORD, contrary to his command. So fire came out from the presence of the LORD and consumed them" (vv. 1–2).

Ian immediately had his issues with this: "Instant death for one transgression? Isn't that a bit extreme? Would a *just* God do something like this? Why is it so important to God that every aspect of worship be done exactly *his* way? Does it really matter which fire these guys used to light their incense burners with? In short, what's the big deal?" But his bigger question was, what in the world possessed these men to behave so idiotically?

Maybe I'm just a pansy, but if I was a priest in that setting and was standing there near a tent wherein you can see a roaring nebula of swirling smoke and flame, *there is no possible way* I would be going in there unless God specifically commanded me to do so, and I'd certainly be taking great pains to follow whatever his instructions were to the tiniest detail even if I did have to go in.

Walter's reply suggested that maybe the two renegade priests weren't so much idiotic as they were arrogant:

In Exodus 24, the two priests accompanied Moses and Aaron up Mount Sinai and had a close encounter of the divine kind. They had the green light to enter God's presence. But just because they had some privilege on a previous occasion, they did not have a blank invitation card for any times they wished. In other words, past performance (Exod. 24) doesn't guarantee future results (Lev. 10).

Still, if the punishment should fit the crime, then it's a stretch to view God's smiting these priests as anything other than cruel and unusual.

Kristen observed that Aaron and his (surviving) sons did not partake of the sin offering (Lev. 10:16–20). When Moses calls him on this, Aaron points out that he'd lost two sons and would God be pleased with him if they ate of the sin offering today? This satisfied Moses.

I read this as Aaron letting loose a little. "Look. I've lost two of my sons. I'm not even allowed to find whatever comfort I can in the grieving rituals. Guess what? I. Really. Don't. Feel. Like. Eating. Now." And Moses accepted that. Finally, thought

I. A little humanity is breaking through here. About time. I did another read-through in my study Bible (it has all the answers at the bottom). That put a different spin on things. The notes said Aaron and his sons don't eat of the offering because they're somehow contaminated by the sin of Nadab and Abihu [the two dead priests]. God and I then had words.

In chapter 24, a man who was a child of a mixed marriage mixes it up with a pedigreed Israelite. In the heat of the scuffle, the biracial man lets loose a cussword with God's name in it (a violation of the third commandment). Immediately the foul-mouthed man is hauled off to Moses for blaspheming God's name with a curse (v. 11). Now when I was growing up, saying a cuss-word with God's name in it got you grounded, but here in Leviticus the ground gets you. Moses waits for the Lord to pronounce sentence, which the Lord does, saying, "Whoever curses his God shall bear his sin. Whoever blasphemes the name of the Lord shall surely be put to death. All the congregation shall stone him" (24:15–16 esv).

Brian's response was something like Ian's: "Yo! That's pretty serious. Put to death? Stoning? No wonder the Israelites and even modern Jews took such reverence in avoiding uttering the name of the Most High. Unfortunately, somehow this has failed to translate so well to modern Christians, and maybe more aptly to me. You should hear me when I drive."

Disturbing stuff, especially since it implies that cursing God and arrogance are as bad as sexual immorality, which also implies that we're all probably in more trouble than we thought. Holiness is very serious business. If I am comforted by anything, it is by the fact that God passed judgment instead of his people doing the judging. It's comforting because God is perfect in justice, but also because God can perfectly judge as to motive; he can see our hearts. But then I think of what goes on in my heart and there goes my comfort.

OVERDOING IT?

Yet the issue of proportionate justice nags. In Leviticus 24, God frames blasphemy in the context of "eye for eye" (v. 20). "Eye for eye" was another way of saying let the punishment fit the crime. Nobody literally poked out another's eye if their own eye was injured, but the law did make sure proper recompense and compensation occurred. At the same time, the law also saw to it that punishment never exceeded what was deserved. But then why does the blasphemer lose his life? Shouldn't the punishment have been curse for curse? Should not God have simply bad-mouthed the blasphemer back?

Leaving aside that to be cursed by God is to die, Leviticus places blasphemy alongside murder, implying that to curse is to kill; that it is somehow claiming God's right to punitive power for yourself (24:16–17; Matt. 5:22). This is one of those harsh Old Testament passages that make you really glad there's a New Testament. Except when you turn to Acts 5 and you read again about that couple collapsing on the spot for deceiving God about a real estate deal (lying to God is just another kind of blasphemy). Jesus could forgive adultery (John 8), but even he said that anyone who blasphemes the Holy Spirit can never be forgiven (Mark 3:29). This helps explain why perjury is so serious. You not only lie under oath, but the oath under which you lie is an oath you took in God's name. The shadows of Leviticus loom (Lev. 27; Matt. 5:37).

Words have power. The Bible enjoins us in worship to "bless the Lord," which when you think about it is an odd notion. How can one confer blessing on the One who is the source of all blessing? The answer may imply that to curse God is such a powerful thing it could actually have an effect on the Almighty himself. If this is true, then the power it has to injure those made in God's image is exponential. No wonder the Bible has so much to say against saying too much.

But if "eye for eye" still applies, why does Jesus argue the opposite? "You have heard that it was said, 'Eye for eye, and tooth for tooth.' But I tell you, Do not *resist* an evil person. If someone strikes you on the right cheek, turn to him the other also" (Matt. 5:38–39, emphasis added). We tend to read this as Jesus commanding us to be doormats that people walk all over. Frankly, I prefer the way Today's English Version puts it, "Do not *take revenge* on someone who wrongs you" (emphasis added). Rather than repudiating *proportionate* justice (punishment fitting the crime), I think Jesus forbids *vigilante* justice (taking the law into your own hands—the Greek verb translated "resist" [*anthistemi*] can mean "to set yourself against" or "retaliate").

Taking the law into their own hands was what those clutching rocks tried to do with that adulterous woman in John 8. When confronted by those eager to stone a woman caught in sexual sin, Jesus did not join in their condemnation. Instead, he thwarted their legalistic zeal by famously announcing, "If any one of you is without sin, let him be the first to throw a stone at her" (John 8:7). To their credit, everyone walked away. But the story did not end there. Jesus then turned to the woman and forgave her, because she had sinned too, and then he said to her, "Go now and leave your life of sin" (v. 11). Jesus' move left everyone empty-handed. The legalists dropped their rocks because of their sin; the adulterous woman let loose her sinfulness due to Christ's forgiveness: all were sinners in equal need of grace.

Kim acknowledged this ubiquity, imagining what she would say if her daughter came home and told her that "Nicky" has two moms: "My response had better not be that much different than if she came home and said Nicky's family is buying a bigger house with a swimming pool and a marble fireplace and gold stairs, because only people with gold stairs are cool...."

Likewise, Lisa wondered, "Why is it that I see Christians holding signs with references to Leviticus as they protest gay marriage, but no one is doing the same on Wall Street with passages condemning greed?" There is a tendency among Christians to treat some sins as more sinful than others, often for what might be cultural or political reasons. Thomas, weighing the emphasis in Leviticus itself, added, "If we God-folk across the U.S. proportionally reflected the emphases of Leviticus—six or seven compulsions to care for the immigrant and the alien versus two condemnations of homosexuality—what a different debate we might be having about one or both of them in this country now. And how differently the church might be regarded."

THE BIBLE I BELIEVE SOMETIMES BOTHERS ME

By this point in the experiment, we'd become convinced that God had his reasons for commanding what he did, even if we couldn't readily figure them out or like them once we did. Sexuality has a way of tripping up everybody. It goes to core issues of our identity as humans.

On this topic, Kristi concluded: "I have nothing intelligent to offer."

Kim, however, stepped in and wrote,

I don't know. No, really, I don't know but I have to because I live in this world and have children to teach and guide, and have even gone so far as to take an oath to do that in a godly Christian home to the best of my ability. I am obliged to have an opinion about, and dare I say it, a judgment of homosexuality. Homosexuality is what it is, an abomination. I don't abominate it, you see; it is a noun. I can, however, choose to hate it, tolerate it, or accept it, speaking of homosexuality itself. The homosexual, however, I am instructed to love (Lev. 19:18). That said, it has been my experience that saying, "Hate the sin; love the sinner" is a definite turnoff to everyone, including my kids.

Kim had a point. We're so bad at distinguishing the difference between sinner and sin that we often just end up hating both (and then lying about it).

Despite the befuddlement, Andrew believed that some things were clear:

When one's very identity is being gay, and then you affirm the Bible's condemnation of that act, any effort at "loving the sinner" will always come across as intolerant no matter how you encourage the love. This is a very hard reality. It also moves us to redefine love. Is love the equivalent of acceptance or is it something more? Love is not what you think it is. Love is not what I think it is. Love is not what the world says it is. Love is what God says it is. Love is defined as a part of God's very essence. And if God says that sex cannot be shared between people of the same gender, that statement is love. You are right. "Easy for me to say." But that is the point: it is not about me.

Maybe rather than providing ammunition with which to condemn others, Leviticus was really trying to get us to confront the dark stuff about ourselves. Jesus had something to say about that too: "Why do you look at the speck of sawdust in your brother's eye and pay no attention to the plank in your own eye?" (Matt. 7:3).

Of course labeling homosexuality a "speck of sawdust" may

be understating matters. Traditional Christian ethics have historically advanced the marital template of one man–one woman, asserting that marriage derives from creation itself. Male and female together in relationship somehow best reflect the Creator ("Let us make humankind in our image"—Gen. 1:26 NRSV). The interpersonal love of the marital relationship mirrors the interpersonal love of the Trinity and therefore the "let *us...our*" language of Genesis 1:26.

Some rightly reply that a trinity is *three* persons while a marriage is only two, but trinitarian theology generally conceives of the Trinity in terms of the Father and the Son, with the Spirit being the love personified between them. Since God's love is perfect love, it takes on its own personhood (or something like that). Others will snidely observe that Western icons of the Trinity typically depict two men and a bird and say you really can't get gayer than that. But the love between Father and Son is not homosexual love; that would be incest. It is familial, parent-child love. A parent and child, inasmuch as they share DNA, can be said to be of "one flesh" in ways that marital love compares (Gen. 2:24).

Parental love and marital love are closely related. They both derive from the basic social covenant that God intended for humanity. Marital love modeled after creation participates in God's creativity and productivity in ways that homosexual love cannot. The capacity for human reproduction is impossible aside from the one man–one woman template. And finally, there is participation in God's covenant fidelity. The biblical picture of God as married to his people stresses a mutual faithfulness that, biblically speaking, exists at marriage's core. Thus Jesus says, "What God has joined together, let man not separate" (Matt. 19:6). In this biblical rubric, sex manages to accomplish all three of these aspects. Sex communicates love. Sex allows for procreation. Sex demonstrates fidelity, inasmuch as adultery is defined as sex with someone who is not your spouse. Christians limit sex to one man–one woman–one marriage because that's how God designed it to work.

Granted, such views on sex get the Christians who hold them branded as prudish. These days, modesty and restraint are often relegated to the category of amusing curiosity, if not life-denying pathology. However, being a prude is not so awful. *Prudish* derives from the Latin word for wisdom, from whence also comes the English word *prudent* as in "good judgment" or "common sense." Many consider prudence the mother of all virtue, the only sure road to actual happiness. In American culture, the pursuit of happiness has been declared an inalienable right, but ironically, little has contributed more to *unhappiness* than the futility of the pursuit.

Happiness, it seems, is a continually moving target. As soon as you arrive in its backyard, it's as if the grass has already turned greener somewhere else. Thus ancient theologians and philosophers—from Solomon to Plato, from Aristotle to Aquinas—all advocated the pursuit of *goodness* instead. Happiness, as it turns out, is a regular by-product of goodness. As most people know from experience, there follows an undeniable contentment from doing the right thing.

BE A PRUDE

Doing the right thing is much more than merely *not* doing the wrong thing. To avoid sin is still to give undue attention to it. You can only go around that apple tree so many times before you end up taking a bite. There is a need for virtue, the practical pursuit of goodness. The Proverbs declare, "The prudent understand where they are going, but fools deceive themselves" (14:8 NLT).

We humans have a flair for tricking ourselves into doing only what we fancy. We're masters of rationalization. We conform our perceptions of reality to our own wants and wishes, something Sigmund Freud termed the "pleasure principle": do it if it feels good even if it's *not* good. However, even Freud recognized that while life might be *driven* by such a pleasure principle, you can't actually live it that way. A reality principle is required. Prudence is the reality principle. It cuts through personal bias in order to ground life in the stable soil of *what is* rather than what you want or wish was. Prudence honors limits, consequences, and responsibility. It understands that actions are bound by relationships and the communities wherein they occur and which they inevitably affect. "The simple believe anything, but the prudent give thought to their steps" (Prov. 14:15 TNIV).

Prudence gives no credence to so-called good intention or well-meaning. These are considered merely subtler forms of rationalization and excuse. Instead, prudence deliberates. It weighs its decisions on the balance of goodness, decency, kindness, and honesty instead of on the balance of personal benefit. "All who are prudent act with knowledge, but fools expose their folly" (Prov. 13:16 TNIV). Prudence heeds the voice of conscience and counsel. Friends are crucial, especially ones courageous and loving enough to speak truth; the ones who refuse to put you on pedestals or use you as crutches. And of course, prudence heeds the voice of God. Spirit and Scripture speak the right and the true, both of which are presupposed by the good. However, prudence does not deliberate for deliberation's sake. Rash decisions are considered imprudent (and costly—Lev. 27:3), but so are excessively cautious ones. Sex without marriage is imprudently sinful, but delaying marriage until your relationship is flawless is imprudently ridiculous.

Virtues are not fail-safe formulas but formed habits that develop through practice. Prudence doesn't wait for the big decisions of life. It becomes a *way* of life, a habit rehearsed in the choices of every moment. Prudence is committed to doing the right thing for the right reason—even before the right thing is required. More than *having* to do good, prudence *wants* to do good. It desires the good life. It relishes the happiness that goodness produces.

It was Thomas Aquinas (I think) who argued that imprudence had its origins in unchastity, in the unconditional surrender to sensual temptation that splits prudence in two. With surrender there is no deliberation and no decisiveness, only giving up and giving in. Such capitulation may offer momentary release, but in time it weakens resolve, leading to chronic disappointment, which eventually renders you callous, cynical, bitter, and shallow. And because nobody wants to be around all *that* very long, you end up isolated too. Perhaps this is why those lacking in virtue are often so lacking in love—and why they are so constantly unhappy. For many, such unhappiness derives from the guilt they feel for not doing right.

In the end, a man from the Pacific Northwest logged into the Leviticus Facebook site and contended that God's hatred of all sin makes gays no better than murderers, an idea as ridiculous as it is repulsive in his mind. For a man to love another man is light-years from a man killing another man (crimes of passion notwithstanding, I might note). He could not understand how love could ever be sinful, since the Bible describes God *as* love. Christ is fine, he said, but not Christians. Christians are too engrossed with sex.

Another reader from the Atlantic Northeast offered a rejoinder. He reminded us that Jesus' parable of the good Samaritan showed that loving your neighbor is not about loving people who are easy to love. When you set the commands of Jesus alongside Leviticus, there is no comparison as to degree of difficulty. Jesus is much sterner. And as for being obsessed with sex, he wrote, Christians are no more engrossed with it than the Bible itself. How about circumcision? Couldn't God have made do with a tattoo or a pierced ear? Apparently not. Despite some arguments about the Lord being concerned about genital hygiene, this man believed that circumcision was God's way of saying that every body part ultimately belonged to the Lord. We are not free to do whatever with whomever we please.

PICKING AND CHOOSING

Some years ago, a woman was leaving our church to move to another city. She came to say good-bye and to thank me for all the church had meant to her. She told me how she had been genuinely transformed by the worship and the sermons, how the community had been wonderful as had the entire ministry she had been privileged to participate in—and not only for her, but for her lesbian partner too. While I was glad that our church had been such a good place for them, I had to ask, "You know that our church believes the Bible teaches homosexual practice to be unbiblical?" She said, "Yes, and we believe everything the Bible teaches and try to follow it except for that one thing. In this one area of our life, because we love each other and want to be together, we've decided to throw ourselves on the mercy of God. And if it turns out that our sin is the unpardonable sin, then so be it. We have to be happy."

At first I was annoyed by her cafeteria approach to the Bible, but then I realized, *That's exactly how I deal with my own sins.* Unable, unwilling to stop doing wrong in one area, I compensate by being good in other areas. It's like that rich young ruler who told Jesus he kept all of God's commandments. Jesus challenged him: "If you want to be perfect, go, sell your possessions and give to the poor, and you will have treasure in heaven. Then come, follow me" (Matt. 19:21). But the rich man could not do it. He wanted to keep his money. But at least he kept his integrity by walking away. The disciples, you'll remember, were shocked by this. "Who then can be saved?" they asked. Jesus replied, "With God all things are possible" (vv. 25–26).

In Leviticus 18:1, the Lord says to Moses, "Speak to the Israelites and tell them, 'I am the LORD your God.'" And then in chapter 19, he says, "Be holy because I, the LORD your God, am holy" (v. 2). If the Lord is our God, there are no work-arounds to holiness. To submit to God is to submit to his lordship in every aspect of our lives, even when we don't like it. When Jesus said, "Blessed . . . are those who hear the word of God and keep it" (Luke 11:28 ESV), he was just echoing Leviticus: "If you obey my decrees and my regulations, you will find life through them. I am the LORD" (Lev. 18:5 NLT).

Chapter Eight

Levitical Side Effects
(aka Guilt Trips)

When a person commits a violation and sins unintentionally in regard
to any of the LORD's holy things, he is to bring to the LORD as a penalty
a ram from the flock, one without defect and of the proper value in silver,
according to the sanctuary shekel. It is a guilt offering.
—Leviticus 5:15

I once officiated a wedding where at the rehearsal dinner, I un-intentionally blurted out something really rude. I shouldn't have said what I said. But I said it: very publicly, as the minister, in front of the grandparents, causing great awkwardness and raising all sorts of questions regarding the authenticity of my salvation. I didn't mean to say it. I didn't plan to say it. It was just one of those dumb things that fly out of your mouth before you realize your lip leash is loose.

Needless to say, all other conversation abruptly stopped. I slinked into the bathroom and hid. The wedding did go on the next day, and the couple remains happily married (happier, mind you, since they moved out of state), but I felt horrible. Frantically guilty. I stayed awake all night agonizing over my inability to keep my mouth shut, fretting that I had ruined the entire weekend and disgraced myself, the church, and all of Christendom. At least that's how it seemed to me. Humiliation does that.

Obviously, I had to apologize. Ask forgiveness. *Beg* forgiveness. Offer to give up an appendage or a pint of blood. I crawled to the groom and told him how sorry I was. How guilty I felt. How I hadn't meant it. Could he ever forgive me? Graciously, he did. He told me not to worry about it. We all say stupid things. We were still friends.

The next time I saw him and his wife, around their first anniversary, everything was just fine. They had not banished me from their house or sworn never to speak to me again. We shared dinner with some other friends and talked about the adventures of the first year of marriage. As we reminisced, the conversation shifted to the last time we were all together—*at their wedding*. I nervously laughed along with everyone else over the antics of the weekend. And then it happened. Somebody jokingly brought up my scurrility. The couple went ashen. Their embarrassment returned, as did my shame. I had to apologize all over again. My unintended misspeaking hung out there like an ever-rotting piece of meat for the whole world to smell. I couldn't get away from the guilt.

Leviticus would have demanded I make a sin offering (Lev. 4:2–12). I would have hauled an unblemished young bull to the temple, laid a hand on its head, and had a priest hack it to pieces, splatter its blood seven times in front of the curtain that hid the inner sanctuary, and then spread more blood on the altar outside that sanctuary. The rest would have been poured on the altar base. The priest would have cut the fat from the bull, both kidneys and the covering of the liver, and burned it together on another altar. Then the bull's hide and the rest of the meat, as well as the head and legs, the organs and guts—all of *that* I would have toted outside of town and torched. That would have comprised my apology—*for just one slip of the lips.*

THE ACCIDENTAL SACRIFICE

The thing they never tell you about the sacrificial system is that it only worked on unintentional sin—that is, the bad stuff you did by accident. Do something wrong *on purpose* and no amount of cattle blood could cover your crime. To sin on purpose meant giving up your *own* blood. You'd get kicked out of town, evicted from the community and from the presence of God, and ostensibly stoned. Numbers 15 dictates that he who *deliberately* sinned was to be "cut off; his guilt remains on him" (v. 31). Such severity led one devout Jewish man whom Sokol knew to craft a convenient bypass. He simply labeled all of his transgressions unintentional. "I didn't mean to do it," he told himself over and over and over again.

Unintentional denotes an error or mistake; something you did that you did not predetermine or were not aware you did in the first place. The picture is commonly one of a sheep that has strayed, having lost its way. Yet Kristen rightly struggled with this concept. She wrote, "I'd always learned that 'unintentional sin' was a contradiction in terms. There can be a difference between what is objectively wrong and what carries moral guilt. You certainly can do wrong actions unintentionally—but sin is always, always, always knowing and intentional. If it isn't knowing and intentional, it isn't sin."

Except that according to Leviticus, sin is sin even if you don't know it. Because God has woven his righteousness into the constellation of the universe, violations of that righteousness constitute a wrong even if done by mistake or by accident.

Andrew reconciled it this way:

> If God has revealed in the Torah his will in most every scenario, and if you break a command without knowing it, your main guilt is that *you should have known it*. It is because you were

too lazy or forgetful to learn and know it. I think that is why Jewish tradition only sees that once you are thirteen, you are accountable. So you teach and teach until then when the person turns thirteen, he or she becomes accountable. This puts a heavy burden on parents to teach their children well.

This elicited a somewhat jumbled response from one woman in New Jersey on the Facebook page. She figured that whether you knew you broke a command or not, there was still plenty of room for forgiveness. Surely a couple of lousy sins weren't going to be the end of you. Besides, unintentional sin is tied to someone else's intentional sin—or something like that. She wrote something about wanting a cheeseburger, which meant somebody had to kill a cow, which if it wasn't killed would walk out in the road and cause a traffic accident, so by eating a cheeseburger (which I think was her unintentional sin) she could prevent traffic fatalities. So unintentional sin can have unintended benefits?

Maybe what she meant is that while mistakes happen, they still carry consequences. In chapter 5, Leviticus gives several examples. There's the eyewitness to injustice who keeps his mouth shut when he should have spoken up (v. 1). This is the mistake of carelessly minding your own business. Not getting involved is not loving your neighbor. A second example has to do with brushing up against a dead carcass or touching an unclean creepy thing (v. 2). Coming in contact with the unclean things of this world can defile you even when you don't realize it. Carelessly watch enough violence in the movies or play enough violent video games, and watch your aversion to violence diminish. A third example has a person carelessly promising to do something and then failing to follow through on the promise (v. 4). We do this all the time: "I'll call you tomorrow." "I'll take care of it; don't worry." And then, "Oh, I forgot. I was going to, but something came up." The operative adverb in each example is *careless*—you don't care about God, your neighbor, or yourself. Such lack of love rips at the righteous fabric of personal and community life.

For Mary Frances, the notion of unintentional sin reminded her of the doctrine of original sin. In response to Kristen's earlier post, Mary Frances wrote how she thought of sin as "more than just intentional acts against God. Our whole being is sinful, so therefore by just being alive we are oozing sin. If we are born into this world as sinners, then long before we are able to make conscious choices, we are still sinful in our nature. By the mere fact that we are not God, we are sinful."

Or, at least, we are predisposed to be sinful. Even when we do right. Too often the intentionally *good* stuff we do gets tainted by pride, the desire for recognition, or the expectation of repayment—all of which might be classified as contrary to Jesus' commands. "Be careful not to do your 'acts of righteousness' before people, to be seen by them. If you do, you will have no reward from your Father in heaven" (Matt. 6:1). The early desert fathers, out of respect for the more clandestine side of sin, referred to the renowned seven deadly sins as "eight deadly thoughts." To gluttony, lust, greed, envy, anger, sloth, and pride they added the sin of *vainglory*. Vainglory emerges whenever you feel you are doing all the right things, but rather than thank God for his enablement and grace, you're irritated that nobody notices what a good Christian you are.

A Texas mom drew an analogy from parenting (an analogy often drawn in the Bible). She reminded the Facebook group of the popular definition of sin as that of "missing the mark." She wrote about how her children frequently miss the mark, but not always on purpose. They simply don't know what they're doing sometimes. They don't realize that they're being disobedient. They're just being kids. Not that kids can't intentionally disobey, of course. Simon concurred, saying, "Exactly. We may not have intended for something injurious to happen to our brothers and sisters, but [because of] the fact something injurious did happen, we have to bear some responsibility for that consequence. An example would be the Big Dig cement tile that crashed down and killed the motorist in Boston. [The Big Dig is the name of a massive public works project in Boston.] I doubt the Big Dig commission was intentionally planning to use subpar and defective material so that four tons of concrete and steel beams could crush a little sedan and kill someone. But the fact that it did happen on their watch means that they are now liable to make reparations for it."

Sokol chimed in too:

One thing I have noticed (correctly or not) in Leviticus is that the majority of commandments concern outward behavior. I am reminded of Jesus' words where he says that if you sin in your mind, you have committed sin in your heart—for me these are the most challenging sins. It appears that Leviticus does not do much to address these sins and how to go about sacrificing for them. I suppose the whole burnt offering can be seen as encompassing *all* sins, but given the details concerning the foods, health, and even sexual behavior, it seems that it would not have been too much to address mental sins too.

Kristen agreed: "There is something about not holding grudges, but you're right. It is far more concerned with actions than thoughts. (And while holding a grudge may be a thought, it will certainly spill over into actions soon enough.)"

Simon added,

Leviticus was not intended as an inward-focused discourse on how to live a mentally and emotionally pure life, although if you are doing neither it shows on the outside in a hurry (relevant stories from my own life will overload Facebook's blogging feature, so for the sake of the greater good I will refrain). God wrote this book to the ancient Israelites on how to live as a community and the issues that may come up for these believers living in a community. As such, there are certainly provisions for when someone wrongs someone else (unintentionally or otherwise) and when relationships are twisted (sleeping with your father and/or mother is an example).

My sense is that the reason Leviticus doesn't mention a dichotomy between attitude and action is because there is no dichotomy. Jesus' remarks in the Sermon on the Mount about hate being murder (Matt. 5:22) and lust being adultery (5:28) appear to challenge the idea that to think bad thoughts is less sinful than committing bad deeds. While this is certainly the case in the U.S. courts (and in our own experience), God, who sees the heart, sees no difference. As Sokol wrote, "It is not just your actions, but even your thoughts that matter." And not only in the New Testament. Paul wrote on our Facebook page, "I was doing the Old Testament a disfavor—God is equally concerned with the inner being here too. Psalm 51:16–17: 'You do not delight in sacrifice, or I would bring it; you do not take pleasure in burnt offerings. The sacrifices of God are a broken spirit; a broken and contrite heart, O God, you will not despise.'"

IT REALLY WAS A MISTAKE!

Because Leviticus speaks to unintentional sin, there *must be* genuine occasions when injury toward others genuinely occurs absent of intent. Mistakes do happen. I say *must be* because this happened to me. I committed an unintentional sin during the Levitical month. Normally I would simply let it slide, but Leviticus didn't let me off the hook.

An important pastoral duty required immediate attention, and the minister who normally does these duties was out of town. Usually this would be no problem. We had plenty of pastors who could fill in. And any of us would have done it if nobody else could, but the problem this week was that nobody could. The other pastors' own schedules were unusually full. Still, somebody needed to do it, which meant that somebody's commitments were going to have to be reshuffled.

We figured that the fair way to decide this would be the biblical way—namely, to draw lots, which in our case meant pulling a name out of a hat. So we all wrote our names on cards and placed them into a hat from which we drew the one whose schedule would have to be completely (and inconveniently) rearranged to accommodate this other necessary task. (Okay, the task was a funeral, but I don't want this to sound callous. The deceased was a former church member from many years prior whom none of us on the current staff knew personally and whose family no longer attended.)

For my part I felt relieved, knowing that my best-laid plans could continue without disruption. I emptied the remaining contents of the hat into the trash and discovered to my horror that I had neglected to write my own name on a card. By mistake, my name wasn't in on the drawing.

My knee-jerk reaction in such cases is first to feel bad, but then to take the edge off that bad feeling through rationalization. Here's where labeling something an accident or unintentional proves helpful. If I didn't mean to do it, then it wasn't really my fault. I can't be blamed. It was no big deal. And any other month I might have let it go at that. But as this was my Levitical month, and Leviticus clearly declares every mistake a big deal, I knew that my work-around would no longer work. To call something an accident and make an excuse is not the same thing as atonement. Still, the good thing about unintentional sin, Levitically speaking, is that you do get preferential access to atonement. Make a mistake, and there is a way to make amends for it.

But there is also an irony. The ready remedy Leviticus provides is the one we rarely take. I'm not talking the public sacrifice of a goat or two pigeons, but its modern equivalent: the public confession of our error and reparations for it. Perhaps for the same reasons of busyness, our persistent minimizing of the effects of our actions on others, or our own faithless rationalizations, we don't make things right with God or our neighbor. Reconciliation takes too much time and energy and requires too much courage, even for the small stuff. Genuine remorse and apologies are difficult—especially for sinful people. But Leviticus demands that we act quickly to admit our sin, to remedy our wrongs, and to fulfill our obligations. To do otherwise contaminates not just the people we love but also the communities we inhabit.

In Leviticus 6:2, there's the line about sinning and being unfaithful to the Lord by deceiving your neighbor. Naturally I read this just after I dumped that hatful of names into the garbage. But really, what were the odds that my name would have been drawn? There were eight other names in that hat. Should I just have drawn again? No, I couldn't have done that because the others not drawn had already counted on keeping their own commitments. What was I to do? Leviticus gave me no other option: "He must make restitution in full, add a fifth of the value to it and give it all to the owner on the day he presents his guilt offering. And as a penalty he must bring to the priest, that is, to the LORD, his guilt offering, a ram from the flock, one without defect and of the proper value" (6:5–6).

For me, this meant I had to confess to my colleague whom I had wronged. And since the Levitical month was to be public, I had to film the whole thing. So I took my video camera to my colleague's office and asked if I might have a minute. I aimed the camera and made my confession. You could see the surprise spread across his face. (Ministers rarely confess to one another.) I told him I could do a ram, or two pigeons or a pound of flour (in case I couldn't afford a ram). Or I could do the funeral. He agreed (with Leviticus) that I had not only sinned against him but against everyone and that yes, I should do the funeral and that for my penalty (since sacrificing a ram was illegal in our state and catching two pigeons nigh unto impossible), I could just take him to lunch somewhere they served lamb (since the priests got to eat the leftovers of the reparation offering). And then I could buy him a scotch (which would account for the value-added "fifth").

A Facebook reader from Israel commented that while this story and the accompanying video were funny, the Torah did not dictate lunch—though lunch was a nice tip of the hat to the commandment's spirit. Usually we just say a quick "I'm sorry" and let it go at that. But restitution is part of the law, and the law reveals the character of God.

I appreciated the affirmation. Even though I now had to readjust all my own plans, and I went above and beyond the commandment by taking my colleague to lunch, *I felt great.* I knew that letting him take the funeral and cancel all his appointments would have left me with a nagging burden of guilt. When we know the right thing to do and don't do it, there's always a sense of loss. There's a lessening of who we know God has redeemed us to be. There's also loss in our relationship with the one we have wronged. We live in a society that assuages guilt by labeling it unhealthy and unnecessary. We're told to forget about it, forgetting as well the hurt and harm we cause other people.

We also forget the hurt and harm we cause God. Leviticus describes our offerings as providing purification, which we normally think of as providing purification for ourselves. But note that the blood of the sacrifice is sprinkled on the altar of the tabernacle—the very symbols of God's presence. God himself has been contaminated by our wrongdoing. But we don't have to live with that. We can fix it. Leviticus points the way. Confess your sin and make things right. Repent, restore, and reconcile. Not only is it the right thing to do, but obediently doing it can bring unexpected happiness.

Restitution is a crucial step in repentance, not only because it repays the victim but because it displays genuineness. And that's no small thing. The next day, my colleague told me he'd do the funeral anyway. He'd actually decided this earlier, and as soon as he did, the conflicting appointments on his schedule canceled themselves. God sort of worked things out. (Though he said I still had to buy him lunch—even if God didn't command it.)

But what if I'd left my name out of that hat on purpose? What does Leviticus say about *deliberate* sin? Nothing. The Levitical system had no provision for forgiving intentional sin. Intentional sin was like premeditated murder—you knew it was wrong, but you deliberately did it anyway. To defy the law in such blatant fashion meant no access to the law for remedy. You could run a veritable Noah's ark full of bulls and flocks through the sacrificial chipper on a daily basis and never squeeze a drop of mercy out of the whole bloody mess. This stern judgment is what prompted the author of the New Testament book of Hebrews to write, "It is *impossible* for the blood of bulls and goats to take away [deliberate] sins" (10:4, emphasis added). If it had, the author of Hebrews asks, wouldn't the Israelites have knocked off the sacrifices? Wouldn't their feelings of guilt have stopped? But as it was, sacrifices persisted, and so did their sin—to the point where even God couldn't stand being around his people any longer. By the time of the prophet Ezekiel, God had had enough and left the building. He abandoned the temple (Ezek. 10). If the Most Holy God was ever to dwell among his unholy people again, something would have to give.

WHAT GIVES?

If your view of God is not a particularly high one; that is, if your tendency is to see God as "the big guy in the sky" rather than the awesome, fearful most holy Author of the universe who dwells in unapproachable light, then chances are you'll simply write off the whole sacrificial slaughterhouse as a primitive, revolting, barbaric, and nauseating enterprise. Which it was. But the reason it was so revolting, barbaric, and nauseating was because human sin is revolting, barbaric, and nauseating to God. (And that's just the unintentional stuff.) As Kim put it (speaking for us all), "I am a poster child for grace. I need it and need it bad."

This is where the Christian gospel comes in. Something had to give, so God gave himself in Jesus as the sufficient sacrifice for both the deliberate sins and whatever you do by mistake. The enormous mass of cattle blood and guts sacrificed throughout the centuries merely hinted at the enormous sacrifice of himself that God would make to save your soul and change your life. But this does not negate the Levitical law. It only affirms its beauty. Having been saved out of Egypt, the Israelites were already God's people when God gave them Leviticus. It was by grace they were saved, through faith. The law was given to guide them into maturity of faith, to show them how to live a saved life. Rather than causing guilt, God's mercy motivates our making amends.

Despite the gospel's good news about intentional sin, Kristen suspected that her Jewish consultants had other ideas ("Call me clever that way"). In her mind, living Levitically had to take into account a Jewish perspective (thus her "consultants"—see chapter 4). We Christians can sometimes skew Old Testament teaching too much to fit our own categories. Kristen summarized her consultants' report on intentional sin this way:

> The general rule for addressing sin is repentance, addressing the results of your sin if possible, and resolving to do better in the future. This doesn't work for unintentional sins because they're likely stuff you don't even know that you did, so you can hardly directly set things right, nor can you reasonably say, "I'm going to try really, really hard not to do this again even though I didn't even know I was doing it the first time." So you need some sort of catchall. "Oh and for anything else I did, I'm sorry for that too so here's a blanket compensation." For intentional ones, you don't get off quite so easy. Slaughtering a bull won't help the person you injured—you need to address that situation and set it right (if possible), as appropriate for the particular case. But that certainly doesn't mean that no restoration is possible for intentional sins. Judaism is all about grounded pragmatism.

A reader from Nashville heartily agreed with Kristen's consultants. He wrote that Jesus himself spoke out of the Old Testament prophetic tradition calling for a cease-fire when it came to killing animals for sin in exchange for a collective sincerity of heart. The last thing Israel needed was more rituals. What Israel needed was more repentance and genuine restoration. He noted that the Hebrew word *kippur* (as in Yom Kippur) could be translated as "cover up." How about instead of covering up our sins, we bring them out into the open for the sake of forgiveness and rededication to God? No animal blood is required for that. Instead, we give our own blood—by which he meant our whole lives—as our pledge to live better.

Kristen replied that she couldn't help but be reminded of "Zacchaeus, the extortionist tax collector who had committed tons of intentional sins. Jesus comes into his house and *boom!*—repentance, restoration of what he unjustly took (plus a hefty penalty), and a changed life" (Luke 19:8).

Kristi appreciated the mention of Zacchaeus. She wrote,

I see such mercy in Jesus' initial statement to Zacchaeus, who was so eager to just see who Jesus was that he climbed a sycamore tree. In climbing the tree, I sense he didn't imagine meeting or touching Jesus was a possibility, or he wasn't prepared for it or was afraid of such an encounter, thus climbing a tree (creating distance and anonymity) rather than fighting through the crowd to get to him. Jesus more than exceeded his expectations. Despite the huge crowd, Jesus speaks such personal words to him, as if they had already been acquainted: "Zacchaeus, come down immediately. I must stay at your house today" (Luke 19:5). Jesus is so unexpected in his actions and words. And he interacts with us in exactly the same way. To put it mildly, he exceeds our expectations (well, mine, anyway).

If only I could exceed my own expectations. I saw a dog on a leash today that seemed far more interested in a pile of another dog's poo on the sidewalk (pardon the vulgar example) than he did in continuing his walk on such a beautiful day. Jesus offers me eternal life in his presence (which begins when I start following him and obeying his commands), but instead I often choose to occupy myself with, comparatively speaking, dog poo. I'm so glad he keeps calling me away from that pile of poo, just as he called Zacchaeus out of that tree.

Over the course of the Levitical month, coming face-to-face with the totality of our sin (whether intentional or not) forced a confrontation with the dark side of motivation we had not heretofore been willing to acknowledge. Yet this created a deeper appreciation for the sacrifice of Jesus and the power of grace. As the group gathered for our weekly kosher dinner, one of the Levites let loose some mildly shocking baggage. Wanting the atonement that Leviticus vividly foreshadowed, she chose to trust God and our community of grace to unload her sin. She confessed it. We heard it. Prayed over it. And trusted Jesus to cover it. Her palpable release prodded others to let loose of their baggage too.

The whole thing was a bit disturbing. We take for granted that Christians are still sinners, but not like *this*! And yet, despite the discomfort of hearing these revelations, our confessions were necessary to make. They were unavoidable too. You can't spend a month together mired in the consequences of your bad behavior without talking about the bad behavior itself. But by bringing all that darkness into the light, each of us found not only an empathetic shoulder, but some hope for redemption too—redemption that ultimately came by way of atonement. As you will read, we took an entire Sunday service and turned it into a virtual Day of Atonement (Yom Kippur sans the scapegoat—Lev. 16).

When it comes to deliberate sin and the ensuing guilt, bulls and goats won't fix it. Being good won't do it. Promising to do better next time won't do it either. Besides, trying to be good is only good when there's nothing working against it. Trying to be good mostly just plays to the virtues we already possess. It rarely gets rid of our vices. That requires repentance and grace.

Simple reflection on the costly extravagance of God's grace should guarantee you never take it for granted. Jesus went nuts whenever anyone did. He told a parable of a master who, while settling accounts with his servants, came across one who owed him an exorbitant amount of money, so much that he'd never be able to pay it back (Matt. 18:23–35). Judiciously, the master was about to toss the servant's wife and kids into jail as collateral when the servant begged for just a *little* mercy. The master shockingly responded with a *ton* of mercy, canceling the servant's entire debt and letting his wife and kids go free.

Inexplicably, however, the pardoned servant later came across a friend who owed him a measly couple of bucks. But rather than extending to his buddy the same grace he had just received from his master, the servant started choking his friend when he couldn't pay up and then threw him into jail! When news got back to the master, he went ballistic. The master furiously handed over the selfish servant to be tortured until he paid up all that he owed (which presumably, being in jail, he never could). Jesus then delivered the gotcha: "This is how my heavenly Father will treat each of you unless you forgive your brother from your heart" (Matt. 18:35).

I returned to the house of my married friends again, many years after their wedding and my stupid comment. We shared dinner with some other friends and caught up on the adventures of life since we'd last been together. As we reminisced, the conversation shifted to their wedding again. And again, someone jokingly brought up that regretful moment. I braced for the repercussions: the embarrassment, the shame, the apologizing all over again, the guilt like rotting meat back on display. But instead my friends only looked at each other quizzically. They honestly couldn't remember what I'd said. So instead, we went on to talking about the good things we *could* remember.

I would tell what it was that I said, but I can't remember it either.

Chapter Nine

Loading the Goat

The goat chosen by lot as the scapegoat shall be presented alive before the
LORD to be used for making atonement by sending it into the desert as a
scapegoat.
—Leviticus 16:10

After several weeks, many experiences, and ample documenta-
tion, the Living Leviticus Facebook group had become a veritable
seminary course on the intricacies and pratfalls of Old Testament
obedience. Interestingly, an Old Testament professor from Bethel
Seminary used our project as part of a required four-credit Old
Testament class (the word *required* being very Levitical).[1] The professor grew out his hair and beard and abstained from meat. One
student returned all borrowed items to their owners (Lev. 25:13),
as well as kept Sabbath, obeyed all traffic laws, and stopped looking at Internet porn.

Both professor and students were surprised by how hard the
assignment turned out to be, which was the complaint of one
of our Facebook site readers. She wrote that she had watched
all the videos and read all the posts and followed all the con-

versations, but the Leviticus project still made no sense to her. Why would Christians want to follow laws and commandments that made the Jewish people in the Bible miserable? Isn't that why God gave the Holy Spirit? Why go back to trying to follow all the commandments if the Spirit renders them obsolete? Jesus obeyed the law for us. She asked whether our church even read the Bible. Did we believe what it says? If so, why bother with Leviticus?

My answer was that yes, we do read and believe the Bible, which is why we bother with Leviticus. Leviticus is in the Bible. And as for following the commandments, it was Jesus himself who said, "If you love me, you will obey what I command" (John 14:15). What did Jesus command? As far as I can tell, most of it is straight out of Leviticus. The word *obey* derives from the verb meaning "to hear"; ergo, to hear Jesus' teaching means nothing if you don't *do* what he says. It takes more than knowing a password to get into heaven. Jesus didn't fulfill the law so that we wouldn't have to obey it. He fulfilled it so that our *failure* to obey it wouldn't be the end of the story.

CLOSING THE GAP

For its first fifteen chapters, Leviticus generally addresses proper worship—how to approach a righteous and holy God. In chapters 17 through 27, Leviticus addresses proper ethics—how to live as righteous and holy people. We're all familiar with the distance that often exists between the two. You go to church and fill the room with your praise and prayer, only to leave church and fail to love your neighbor or refuse to love your enemy, the very things the God you just worshiped commands you to do. Jesus rightly asks, "Why do you call me, 'Lord, Lord,' and do not do what I say?" (Luke 6:46).

This distance between hearing and doing is what's often labeled *sin*. The Old Testament provides a varied vocabulary to describe it: *rebellion, infidelity, disloyalty, disobedience, getting dirty, wandering, trespassing, transgressing,* and *missing the mark.* And yet sin is a perversity that pollutes God even more than it pollutes us. If God is indeed infinite in nature, any transgression against his nature amounts to an infinite transgression. Therefore merely amending our lives and promising to do better isn't enough. The only way to span the distance between our worship and our failure to live as we worship—between God's expectations in Leviticus 1–15 and their implications in Leviticus 17–27—is with chapter 16. Atonement.

For those who are Jewish, the Day of Atonement, or Yom Kippur, is the holiest day on the calendar. Once a year, everybody gets their sin taken care of over the course of an exhausting twenty-five hours of prayer and abstinence from work, food, drink, sex, bathing, and leather shoes. (I understand that the prohibition against leather shoes has to do with not wanting to be presumptuous by appearing before God shod in the skins of a slaughtered sacrificial animal.) Yom Kippur is spent sitting in synagogue as a long list of sins is confessed aloud. Even if you haven't committed one of the sins read from the list, you still confess it. Jewish tradition teaches that each person bears a certain measure of responsibility for sins committed by others, since everybody is part of the same community. The people of God are supposed to watch after each other.

While all this contrition and confession (and accountability) may sound depressing (and overwhelming), the Talmud labels Yom Kippur as the holiest but also one of the *happiest* days of the year. It's the same reason its Christian counterpart is ironically called Good Friday. Atonement means your sins are forgiven. The slate is clean. It's a happy day.

WE'VE COME A LONG WAY

These days, neither the Christian Good Friday nor the Jewish Yom Kippur looks much like Leviticus 16. There are no animals sacrificed, no scapegoats chased off into the wilderness, no mercy seat on which to splatter blood. However, for the ancient Israelites, all of this was necessary to purge the tabernacle of a year's worth of pollution due to their unholiness and impurity. Perhaps you're thinking, *How could there be any sin left to pollute the tabernacle with all of the blood of those innocent animals running through the sacrificial system every day?* Remember, the sacrificial system only took care of *unintentional* sin. Intentional, deliberate sinners weren't allowed to sacrifice, so the stain of their offenses remained in God's face and got all over his house. Therefore, once a year, on the Day of Atonement, the high priest risked his life to purify the sanctuary. Confronting the Most Holy God with the sins of the people was very dangerous. Nevertheless, purification of the sanctuary proved necessary in order that those who could sacrifice would have their sacrifices accepted. The gory details of Atonement Day reminded everyone of the unintentional sin they'd both remembered and neglected to confess. Moreover, because the temple was modeled after creation, Atonement Day drove home the reality that human sin polluted more than human life and God's nature; it spewed its toxic waste all over heaven and earth too.

Approaching God with your sin was very risky business, but failing to do so was worse. In Leviticus 26, God warns,

> If you will not listen to me and carry out all these commands, and if you reject my decrees and abhor my laws and fail to carry out all my commands and so violate my covenant, then I will do this to you: I will bring upon you sudden terror, wasting

diseases and fever that will destroy your sight and drain away your life. You will plant seed in vain, because your enemies will eat it. I will set my face against you so that you will be defeated by your enemies; those who hate you will rule over you, and you will flee even when no one is pursuing you.

If after all this you will not listen to me, I will punish you for your sins seven times over. (vv. 14–18)

Kristi experienced what she considered to be a dose of Leviticus 26. She and Kristen had been throwing around the term *smiting* for most of the month, but so far neither she nor Kristen, nor any of the rest of us, had reported being the direct object of the Lord's displeasure (thank Jesus). At least not until Kristi's episode. She made a list of potential offenses from Leviticus 19 and recalled corresponding behaviors that violated each:

1. *Lying and deception* (Lev. 19:11). While on the phone with my friend Erin I was simultaneously checking our Living Leviticus website when she asked me to go to another website to share something with her. I said, "Hold on…my computer is really slow." That's not true. I just didn't want to switch websites. I confessed immediately (well, there was a five-second delay—she was very kind in quickly forgiving me). And let's throw pride in there as well because I was on this website checking for glaring grammatical errors in one of my posts.

2. *Slander* (Lev. 19:16). A woman yelled at, cursed at, and belittled me because she felt offended by my actions a few days ago. Upon relating the story to my small group, I definitely did so attempting to underscore not only the "piety" of my intentions in relating to her, but also the "absurdity" of her reaction.

3. *Vengeance-taking and grudge-bearing* (Lev. 19:18). This one is really bad. I was driving with three kids in the backseat and had been searching twenty minutes for a parking space. A nanny with her three kids began to cross at the crosswalk, despite her no-walk signal, just as I was approaching the green right turn arrow (that only lasts for ten seconds, by the way). Well, I waited impatiently for them to cross, called her an idiot under my breath, and turned the corner just hastily enough for her to sense my annoyance. Who's the idiot?
4. *Breeding together two kinds of cattle* (Lev. 19:19). Okay, I didn't do this one, though I'm sure I could think up an equivalent offense if I tried hard enough.
5. *Not observing and doing all statutes and ordinances* (Lev. 19:37). Self-explanatory. If I haven't kept 1–4, then I have failed to keep "all statutes and ordinances." I find it amusing that God not only gives us individual commands to obey, but also reminds us (in a command of its own) to keep all the commandments he's already given.

Now on to the smiting. Kristi wrote,

Last night, after a very healthy [and kosher] dinner of fish and vegetables, my stomach started feeling a bit queasy. Then an hour later I thought, *Something is certainly amiss here. But what could it be? Is there a bug going around? No way is it food poisoning.* I went to bed at 10:30, convinced that a little sleep would fix everything. Two hours later, feeling horrible, the bathroom and I had our first intimate visit of what turned out to be many as I was attacked by Levitical affliction in all its horror. The next seven hours were agonizing, excruciating, abysmal—you get the picture. It felt as if dementors were trying to suck my soul from my body. Seriously. I fail to remember a sickness having such a profound effect on me. My inner dialogue went from *It's just a stomach bug, you pansy, quit complaining* to *God, please, PLEEEEASE take me now! I can't go through this again! AAAAHHHHH!*

Kim, a mother of two, commented that she'd had food poisoning once, and giving birth was less agonizing.

Kristi went on,

> I contemplated sleeping in the bathroom. It was pitiful. Now I think it was just a stomach bug and not God smiting me. But it *felt* like a smiting. God declares in Leviticus 26:14–18, "If you do not obey Me and do not carry out all these commandments,...I will appoint over you a sudden terror, consumption and fever, [and I] will punish you seven times more for your sins" (NASB). If you ask me, that description strangely resembled last night's experience.

In fairness to Leviticus 26, the smitten in verses 14–18 are those who *reject* and *abhor* the law, strong verbs that denote strong contempt for the commandments. These are people who have turned away from the Lord; God has not turned away from them. In the end, God gives them what they want—which carries a two-fold meaning. It's like the guy who walks into a bar and asks for a double entendre, so the bartender *gives it to him.* Yet the curses in Leviticus 26 are severe for a reason. The severity serves as yet another warning to not take God's grace for granted.

SCAPEGOATING

Sin defiles not only individuals, but communities, institutions, earth, and heaven too. For the ancient Israelites, their conduct was inextricably tied to the holiness of God's house. When they were faithful, the sanctuary radiated their commitment. When they were unfaithful, the sanctuary reflected their failing. If it was not cleansed, God threatened to depart and leave the community to its futility—a threat that he carries out once we get to Ezekiel.

For reasons only humans can rationalize, the Israelites presumed upon God's presence. It wasn't that they ignored it; they flouted it. They crafted idols of stick and stone and praised them instead. They severed themselves from the ethos of the law. They desecrated the temple, they exploited the poor, they engaged in lascivious acts of sexual pleasure and called it worship, they murdered innocent people—all under the presumption of Yahweh's continued favor. So God left the temple, and he left the Israelites to the mercy of Babylon, which had no mercy. The Babylonians annihilated the temple and all but annihilated the people.

But astonishingly, even their near total annihilation didn't impel obedience. As is the case with most human beings, our memories are short. We don't learn our lessons. Therefore even though the temple was rebuilt, God's glory never inhabited it as before. Not until Jesus shows up in the temple himself does God fully return, but then only to announce the building's final demise (Matt. 24:2). Once Jesus departs earth, God's now-totally-vacated house gets totally leveled by the Romans. This is why the Jewish practice of Yom Kippur no longer adheres to Leviticus 16. There's no earthly temple left to cleanse.

In Leviticus, the earthly temple had yet to be built (King Solomon would do that later). Its precursor, the tabernacle, contained the mercy seat, which sat at the center of the Leviticus 16 ritual. The mercy seat was a golden chair of sorts that sat atop the ark of the covenant, where it functioned as the boundary line between God's holiness and human unholiness. It was adorned with two statues of cherubim (angels) on either end, their wings touching in the middle.

Enthroned between the cherubim, within the Holy of Holies, God appeared in a cloud to accept the atoning sacrifices offered by the high priest. The high priest would be freshly showered for purification, dressed in a sacred linen tunic, turban, and sash, with linen underwear to boot. Lest the high priest glance at God and die, incense was burned to screen him from peeking. He took a young bull and a young ram and hacked them up as a sacrifice for his own sin (no matter how many bulls and rams he'd already hacked up for those sins before). The sacrificial blood from the bull and the ram was sprinkled on the mercy seat to purify it too and then sprinkled seven times in front of the mercy seat to reconsecrate it for holy use. Then the people were purified in order to approach God for their forgiveness (atonement is a multilayered affair).

The priest brought forward two goats and drew straws in order to determine which one died on the spot for the sake of purification (16:9) and which one became the scapegoat (v. 10). Afterward, from behind the curtain that shielded the congregation, the high priest emerged liturgically loaded with the people's impurities (their sins that polluted the sanctuary) and their iniquities (their sins that polluted themselves). Then with both hands, the high priest transferred all this wickedness and rebellion onto the live (but doomed) scapegoat (v. 21). The scapegoat was carried far out of town and chased away, thereby hauling all of their toxicity out into the wilderness to dump it. Later Judaism would go so far as to push the scapegoat off the edge of a gorge so as to assure its elimination. Nobody wanted a year's worth of wickedness finding its way back into town. Nevertheless, even for those of us who have experienced God's grace and forgiveness, it is as if we each have our own personal and pesky scapegoat that keeps finding its way back anyway, unloading our sin back onto us all over again.

Simon decided to take stock of his own holiness over the course of a seven-day accounting where he judged his thoughts and deeds of each day as either "holy" or "unholy." He wrote,

> No day existed in which the holy items outnumbered the unholy items. Not only are there very few holy items in total, but they are offset by some horrendously unholy things, sometimes separated by mere hours in the same day. Items marked *Holy* tended to be ordinary, core Christian values that I should be living already and are not heroic by any stretch of imagination. Items marked *Unholy*, however, were spectacular to behold—in the same way that a train wreck can happen in a thousand ways, each more spectacular than the one before.
>
> To make myself feel better, I made an attempt at detecting unholy things that other people may be doing (just trying to keep an honest scale, in accordance with Leviticus 19:36). However, the Lord was not at all interested that I keep records of other people's wrongdoings. Instead, he kept bringing up all the things for which I alone am responsible.
>
> Living by Leviticus has been like standing naked in front of a mirror—not only are your sins exposed, but you're not allowed to look at anybody else's sins just so you can change the focus for a second.

RENT-A-GOAT

The need for atonement is so palpable that we were tempted to rent a couple of goats for our own Day of Atonement. We thought that watching our souls get purified (by the dead goat) and carried away (by the scapegoat) might make grace more real. Of course, renting a couple of goats was one thing. Finding somebody to rent us two goats to sacrifice and chase away was something else. And even with the scapegoat that drew the lucky(?) straw, you still had the problem of giving the goat back to its owner with our collective sins loaded up on it (unless it died in traffic after we chased it out of church). Somebody suggested that perhaps one of us Levites could just dress up like a goat. But you still have the same problem: who in their right mind would give themselves for the sins of everybody else?

I mean, except for Jesus. He is our scapegoat. As we hear intoned from Isaiah every Good Friday: "We all, like sheep, have gone astray, each of us has turned to his own way; and the LORD has laid on him the iniquity of us all" (53:6). "God made him who had no sin to be sin for us," Paul wrote to the Corinthians (2 Cor. 5:21). And then to the Romans: "All have sinned and fall short of the glory of God, and are justified freely by his grace through the redemption that came by Christ Jesus. God presented him as a *sacrifice of atonement*" (Rom. 3:23–25, emphasis added). Or as other translations have it, *"a propitiation by his blood*, to be received by faith" (v. 25 ESV, emphasis added). Interestingly, if you trace the English word *propitiation* back through the Latin translation of the Greek translation of the Hebrew Bible, you get to the word in Leviticus 16 translated "mercy seat." Not only does Jesus become our scapegoat, but he is our mercy seat too. He dies at that boundary line where God's holiness meets human unholiness and atonement gets made for good.[2]

The book of Hebrews picks up on the Levitical imagery of atonement by naming Jesus as our heavenly high priest (8:1). Whereas the Levitical high priest annually risked his life to purify the sanctuary and the people, when Christ came as high priest, he *gave* his life. Jesus is both the priest and the sacrifice. Hebrews declares that Jesus "entered the Most Holy Place once for all by his own blood, having obtained eternal redemption....How much more, then, will the blood of Christ, who through the eternal Spirit offered himself unblemished to God, cleanse our consciences from acts that lead to death, so that we may serve [read *obey* here] the living God!" (9:12, 14).

Here the earthly temple is understood to be a mere replica of the real temple, which is in heaven. Whereas the Levitical high priest had to enter the replica annually to make atonement, atonement in the real (eternal) temple only had to happen one time (ergo "eternal redemption" —Heb. 9:12). Moreover, what the New International Version translates as "acts that lead to death" (v. 14), other translations render "dead works" (NASB) or even "useless rituals" (TEV).

Brian, who like the rest of us struggled with living by so many parts of Leviticus that felt like useless ritual, wrote how "living by the letter of the law can be hollow and feel mechanical...but the danger of living by the spirit is that one can get focused on trampling on God's process (as someone said, I treat God as if he's *my* friend rather than being *his* friend), eventually seeking unfair justifications for one's behaviors or actions." Mary Frances agreed. She noted that "a focus on spirit (freedom) over law (ritual) allows Christians to easily slide past a multitude of sins, both literally and figuratively, that we should actually be duking out with God."

Brian, viewing "spirit" as grace and "truth" as the need for repentance to get that grace, went on to recall how Jesus tells the woman at the well in John 4,

> "Believe me, woman, a time is coming when you will worship the Father neither on this mountain nor in Jerusalem....A time is coming and has now come when the true worshipers will worship the Father in spirit and truth, for they are the kind of worshipers the Father seeks. God is spirit, and his worshipers

must worship in spirit and in truth" (vv. 21, 23–24). Do we worship in both spirit and truth?

Kristen took up Brian's question:

Do we worship in both spirit and truth? In my life, sometimes yes, very often no. And I think that's okay. Maybe I should explain. Sometimes the sun is shining, the birds are singing, God's in his heaven, and all is right with the world. Prayers of thanksgiving are easy and joyous. Here we are, worshiping in spirit and in truth. But sometimes my spiritual engine is not exactly firing on all cylinders. I'm tired and cranky and if I were simply to offer God what's in my heart, it would be, "I'm tired and cranky and going back to bed." Or something like that. The value of ritual is that it tells me what to do at those times. It can be just going through the motions, but these are good motions, and over time they start to sink in and shape the motion-er.

Is going through the motions like that really worshiping in spirit and in truth? Maybe not. But if I consistently and deliberately open up that space for the Spirit to work in my life, over time my worship will become more spiritual and truthful—even if I can't articulate quite how that all is happening. That's the individual level. There's also the community level. These motions can be a big part of how we are bound together. We aren't a bunch of individuals communing with God in our own separate ways but a people who come to God together. I might not be in a real "Gloria" frame of mind right now—but maybe you are, and the "Gloria" gives me words to share in your joy. And I might be in the depths—but what affects me affects you too, so you join me in the prayer of confession. Ideally we'd be able to infuse all this with sincere passion. And don't get me wrong, often that's exactly what happens. But the

world's a mess and we're a mess and often it doesn't. Going
through the motions can still be a move in the right direction.

Kristi gave Kristen a hearty *amen*. She wrote how great it
is to be in community such that "your strength makes up for
my weakness and vice versa. I think that's an important aspect
of the history of God's dealing with his people that we often
overlook. In fact, I've never considered my own salvation in that
light."

ESCAPEGOATING

While the Levitical Day of Atonement ritual no longer occurs
in the temple (since there is no longer a temple), the need for
atonement in the context of community remains. Thus Jews still
solemnly observe Yom Kippur, and most Christians commemo-
rate Good Friday. I say *most* Christians, since I know plenty of
believers for whom any time spent somberly remembering the
crucifixion is considered time wasted. For these Christians, Easter
trumps Good Friday and with it any need to fixate on sin and
guilt. I've heard it preached, "Jesus suffered and died so that you
don't have to." Pain and suffering, and even sin for that matter
(at least the sin that *did* matter), were for unbelievers. Real Christians didn't sin anymore; we merely *transgressed*. (This sounds a
lot like the Jewish man who conveniently labeled all his sins "unintentional.")

Even the Christians who take Good Friday seriously don't
necessarily want to heed what serious observance demands. Re-
cently, a local archbishop refused to relax the fasting requirement
(no meat) for Roman Catholic Red Sox fans who had requested a
special dispensation since Opening Day fell on Good Friday. For
attending Catholics, this meant no hot dogs, sausages, or pepper-

oni pizza—a sacrifice, some fans said, too great to make. A radio reporter suggested to devout Roman Catholic Sox fans: "Just eat your hot dog on Friday and go to confession on Saturday." Easy enough since confession no longer demands your prized livestock.

Still, confession must not be *that* easy. Three-quarters of American Catholics either don't participate in confession at all, or go less than once a year. In the Boston area, more than 80 percent of Catholics don't even attend church regularly.[3] Nevertheless, for Christians (both Catholics and Protestants) to access atonement and reconciliation with God, confession is required (even if confession *booths* are not). Atonement is not automatic. As the apostle John put it, "If we claim to be without sin, we deceive ourselves and the truth is not in us. If we confess our sins, he is faithful and just and will forgive us our sins and purify us from all unrighteousness" (1 John 1:8–9). The language of confession and purification is pure Leviticus.

Holy Week came on the heels of our Levitical month, and thus it seemed proper as an outcome of our experiment to offer to our congregation the best approximation of the Day of Atonement we could muster—namely, a liturgy of confession and purification. I borrowed the Anglican liturgy of penitence (striking a balance as it does between Catholic and Protestant), and invited the congregation at our services to load their sins on the scapegoat. The liturgy went something like this:

MINISTER: Holy God, Holy and Mighty, Holy Immortal One, have mercy upon us. Enlighten our hearts that we may remember in truth both our sins and your unfailing mercy.
PEOPLE: Amen.
MINISTER: Hear the Word of God to all who truly turn to him.
"Come unto me, all ye that travail and are heavy laden, and I

will refresh you" (Matthew 11:28). "God so loved the world, that he gave his only begotten Son, to the end that all that believe in him should not perish, but have everlasting life" (John 3:16). "This is a true saying, and worthy of all to be received, that Christ Jesus came into the world to save sinners" (1 Timothy 1:15). "If anyone sins, we have an Advocate with the Father, Jesus Christ the righteous; and he is the perfect offering for our sins, and not for ours only, but for the sins of the whole world" (1 John 2:1–2). Now, in the presence of Christ, and of us his people, confess your sins with a humble and obedient heart to Almighty God, our Creator and our Redeemer.

PEOPLE: Holy God, heavenly Father, you formed us from the dust in your image and likeness, and redeemed us from sin and death by the cross of your Son, Jesus Christ. Through baptism you clothed us with the shining garment of his righteousness and established us among your children in your kingdom. But we have squandered our inheritance and have wandered far in a land that is waste. Hear us as we confess these and all other sins we cannot now remember. We turn to you in sorrow and repentance. Receive us again into the arms of your mercy, and restore us to the blessed company of your faithful people. (People then silently confess their sins.)

MINISTER: Will each of you turn again to Christ as your Lord?

PEOPLE: I will.

MINISTER: Do each of you, then, forgive those who have sinned against you?

PEOPLE: I forgive them.

MINISTER: May Almighty God in his mercy receive your confession of sorrow and of faith, strengthen you in all goodness, and by the power of the Holy Spirit keep you in eternal life.

Our Lord Jesus Christ, who offered himself to be sacrificed for us to the Father, and who absolves all sinners who truly repent and believe in him, of his great mercy forgive you all your offenses and restore you to perfect peace: In the name of the Father, and of the Son, and of the Holy Spirit.

PEOPLE: Amen.

MINISTER: Now there is rejoicing in heaven; for you were lost, and are found; you were dead, and are now alive in Christ Jesus our Lord. Abide in peace. The Lord has put away all your sins.

PEOPLE: Thanks be to God.[4]

Many admitted that the experience of corporate, liturgical confession was surprisingly powerful. Kristen summarized it best:

I had a hard time with Leviticus month. For about thirty days and eighteen hours, I groused and complained. My postings were getting progressively darker and darker. It wasn't going well. Early in the month I had been reading through the sacrificial section and was convinced that the modern-day, post-Jesus equivalent is confession. This is something I knew about from my Catholic days but had never been part of my life. I had gone to confession a grand total of once, when I was ten years old. I was not interested in doing this again—but the way I didn't want to do this made me think that I really ought to. I took a deep breath and jumped in.

I don't know what I was expecting, but this was not it. This was large. This was a major life event. I spent hours dredging up the muck in my life and preparing my list—and then it was all washed away. Gone. I was walking on air. And all of a sudden I knew that I was in a really good place and I did not want to muck it up anymore. "Okay, God," I prayed, "this is fantastic. I want to stay here. Whaddya want me to do?" Needless to say, reading through Leviticus again looked so different in the light of grace.

GET YOUR GOAT

Atonement takes away our sin and makes us into holy people—enabling our ethics to square with our worship, people who can preach what we practice. Yet somehow the distance between reality and experience remains. How is it that people made holy by Christ still act so unholy? Part of the problem may have something to do with a flawed understanding of atonement itself. To experience atonement is more than to be declared "not guilty" before God. To experience atonement is to be changed by God. Our tendency is to embrace the former while resisting the latter. We treat "Jesus loves you just as you are" as permission to stay that way. We screw up, say "I'm sorry," and feel bad, thinking this somehow makes up for our unwillingness to heed our new calling and mend our ways. Chronic guilt, as exhausting as *that* is, is still the price we're willing to pay in order to avoid change. And then, since we're already feeling bad, we figure we might as well just keep on doing the junk we're doing. At least that way we can say we're consistent. It's a nasty cycle.

Our friends aren't always a lot of help either. I remember on the occasion of one of my colossal screwups, a Christian friend heard my confession; but rather than doling out the censure I feared (but frankly needed), he compassionately put his arm around me and with a tender look said, "Welcome to the human race." It's interesting that some friends will resist confronting us although it may be what we seriously need. Perhaps the resistance to confront has to do with their desire to avoid being confronted.

I much preferred the response of another good brother.

When I confessed what I had done as I spoke with him over the telephone, he empathized with my regret and sorrow. As a fellow sinner, he understood how we get ourselves into the messes we get ourselves into. But then he asked me whether I had my other hand free. "Sure," I replied. "Okay," he said, "take your free hand and smack yourself upside your head. What were you thinking?"

It's easy to think that since our sins don't rank up there with the truly heinous of history, surely God can't be so concerned. Yet the same book of Leviticus that promises the wrath of God on idolaters (19:4), adulterers (20:10), extortionists (19:13), murderers (24:17), and pedophiles (18:17) assures identical wrath upon those who tell white lies (19:11), bad-mouth their parents (20:9), dislike their neighbors (19:18), or break the Sabbath (23:3). Jesus himself said that the evil you do in your heart counts the same as the evil you do with your hands and mouth (Matt. 5:22, 28; Mark 7:21–23).

God has this thing for total holiness and total purity and total righteousness such that whatever smacks of unholiness, impurity, or unrighteousness—however insignificant it seems and at whatever level it occurs—sends him through the celestial roof. As Leviticus 26:14–18 (with its divine threats of sudden terror, wasting diseases, fever, humiliating defeat, and smiting "as your sins deserve" [v. 21]) makes clear, God is so committed to holiness and righteousness that he'll do whatever it takes to achieve it in his people—*even if it kills him.*

Which it does, of course. After all, that's the gospel. In Levitical fashion, Jesus is the Lamb of God who takes away the sins of the world (Gen. 22:8; Lev. 1:4; John 1:29). The Lamb of God takes *away* the sins of the world by taking *on* the sins of the world. He takes away sin by taking sin *onto* himself; he is our scapegoat. But get this: by taking on "the sins of the world" Jesus takes on both the sins *you commit* and the sins committed *against you*. This has troubling implications. Jesus dies in solidarity with the *oppressed,* but more profoundly, he dies to exonerate their *oppressors*. Jesus suffers the suffering of injustice, but he suffers the suffering of justice too. Christ dies for the sake of the guilty, be they perpetrator or victim. The spotless lamb becomes the black sheep. The troubling implications have nothing to do with Jesus' dying to save you from your sins. I've yet to meet a Christian who isn't thankful to have his or her sins forgiven. The troubling part is Jesus' command to go and do likewise: to suffer the wounds of grace that come with forgiving your enemies.

There remain those who aren't in the mood to heed either Jesus or Leviticus on this front. An exasperated congregant approached me after a related sermon. "Great," he said, "another round of how it's *my* Christian responsibility to be a humiliating doormat for people who've hurt me. Why not a little justice for the victim? A little righteous anger? What's wrong with telling the truth and calling sin a sin and insisting something be done to right the wrong? Doesn't forgiving my enemies only encourage more bad behavior? Why not some condemnation?"

Well, actually, forgiveness is a lot like condemnation. Grace is fundamentally an indictment. Pardon is only extended to those who need it. To forgive is first to blame. My favorite illustration is that of a blind date. Imagine you've been set up. You're met at the restaurant by a person you've never set eyes on before. She walks over and the first words out of her mouth are not "Nice to meet you," but "I forgive you." To have someone forgive you implies that you are not a good person. To have someone be cursed and crucified on a cross for you implies you are a really bad person—"prone to do evil, incapable of good," a sinner "without end or ceasing" "provoking most justly [God's] wrath and indignation," just as the old Communion prayers confess.[5]

Nevertheless, we chafe under the command to love our enemies and pray for our persecutors, begrudging Jesus for making us be doormats (this despite Jesus' letting us walk all over him). Yale theologian Miroslav Volf acknowledges how for victims, forgiveness can feel too much like acting as if the offense never happened. Yet when we forgive, we actually affirm a rightful claim to justice. It's just that we're choosing not to press charges.[6]

Granted, this is fine in principle, but not once we're talking about actual people who've hurt us. If you've ever had someone, perhaps even a close friend, willingly betray your trust by a wrong word or deed, then you know the hurt, the humiliation, and the anger that consume you. Thankfully, in some cases, an offender apologizes and asks for forgiveness, making forgiveness much more doable. But many times there is no repentance, yet we're still told to forgive. This is not fair. So why should we do it? Because Jesus said so (the Levitical rationale shows up in the New Testament too).

Admittedly, forgiveness is not the same as reconciliation. The waiting father forgives his prodigal son, but the parable's not complete until the son returns to his father's embrace. In this way forgiveness works like an invitation. You offer it to invite repentance and reconciliation, but you do so at the risk of rejection. Repentance may be necessary for reconciliation, but repentance does not condition the offer of forgiveness. To offer forgiveness is a one-way deal. Grace is a free gift that attaches no strings. To forgive the unrepentant is not optional for the Christian. It's the heart of the gospel—a gospel for which Jesus says we must suffer (Mark 8:35).

But we do not suffer alone. Forgiveness is borne not of our own strength but of the power and the right of Christ, who died for us while we were yet unrepentant. It is Christ's suffering for us that makes our suffering possible; Christ's forgiveness becomes our own forgiving. Grace turns us into new people. "I have been crucified with Christ," Paul wrote to the Galatians. "It is no longer

I who live, but Christ who lives in me" (Gal. 2:20 ESV). Likewise with forgiveness, "It is no longer I who forgive, but Christ who lives in me." Jesus *in us* forgives *through us*, and that is why and how we forgive.

AS WE FORGIVE OUR DEBTORS

Forgiveness is also helped along if we are members of communities of forgiveness (aka churches). Like corporate confession helps us acknowledge our faults, communities where forgiveness is practiced help us practice forgiveness by allowing us to experience the joy of both receiving and giving grace. Christine the seminary student/Levite made the point that throughout the Bible,

> what applies to the community also applies to the individual within that community, and vice versa. Therefore, as Christians, we cannot interpret God's laws and precepts individually, but as individuals who are part of a collective. What I do as an individual inevitably affects other people. The idea that "what's true for you is not necessarily true for me" is a grave fallacy, since a person's actions, which are based on a person's beliefs, often result in consequences that affect others and thus become true for the others, whether they like it or not.

Some Christians have a nasty tendency to view salvation as solely for our own personal security and benefit. That's even the way we describe it: having a *personal relationship* with Christ. Just me and Jesus. Keeping Jesus all to yourself is like the parable in Luke's Gospel where a farmer scores a bumper crop, but rather than share the bounty, he hoards it. God calls him a fool and strikes him dead, which is how Jesus says it will be for anybody who hoards God's treasures for himself alone (Luke 12:16–21).

Christ "died for all," Paul wrote to the Corinthians, "that those who live should no longer live for themselves but for him who died for them and was raised again" (2 Cor. 5:15). For reasons sometimes hard to comprehend, God so loved the world that he sent his Son to die for it. And for reasons sometimes even harder to comprehend, God so loves the world that he sends his people, you and me, to die to ourselves for the sake of spreading his love: forgiving, feeding the hungry, doing justice, speaking truth with love, not being ashamed of the gospel, caring about somebody else for a change.

Though you can do nothing to earn God's grace, you must nevertheless *do something* to show you've received it. The sixteenth-century Reformer Martin Luther put it like this:

> Although I am an unworthy and condemned man, my God has given me in Christ all the riches of righteousness and salvation without any merit on my part—out of pure, free mercy—so that from now on I need nothing except faith which believes that this is true. Why should I not therefore freely, joyfully, with all my heart, and with eager will do all things which I know are pleasing and acceptable to such a Father who has over-whelmed me with his inestimable riches? I will therefore give myself as Christ to my neighbor, just as Christ offered himself to me.... The outward [grace] that I show in my deeds is a sure sign that I have forgiveness of sin in the sight of God. On the other hand, if I do not show grace in my relations with my neighbor, I have a sure sign that I do not have forgiveness of sin in the sight of God and that I am stuck in my unbelief.[7]

Chapter Ten

Let Us Keep the Feasts

These are my appointed feasts, the appointed feasts of the LORD,
which you are to proclaim as sacred assemblies.
—Leviticus 23:2

Let's face it, despite whatever positive spin I've spun, the book of Leviticus can feel tedious, onerous, and even oppressive—and that's for those who only *read* it. The exacting rules about fabric and food and mildew and skin—it's hardly surprising that the ancient Israelites (and modern Christians) found Leviticus so tough to obey. But then you come to chapter 23 and are struck by an inescapable irony. Leviticus may be the heaviest rule book in the Bible, but among those heavy rules is the command to celebrate heavily. Eight times the Lord instructs his people to party: stop working, strap on the festival feedbag, and enjoy the grace and goodness of God.

Whether our Levites-for-a-month actually experienced this fun side of Leviticus is hard to say. I know that for me, trying to heed all the intricacies of Levitical law left little time for rejoicing. The psalmist sings, "The law of the LORD is perfect, reviving the soul.... The precepts of the LORD are right, giving joy to the heart" (Ps. 19:7–8), but mostly it gave me a headache. Obviously I was missing something. What good is following the law if all it does is make you not want to follow it? Maybe this is why God inserted chapter 23. The Lord fills up the social calendar to make the true joy of obedience unavoidable.

Each of the Levitical feasts is labeled a Sabbath, which means no work—one of the most toilsome commandments for modern American Christians to heed. Our work provides our identity and security. It keeps conversation alive at dinner parties ("So, what do you do?"). Working on holidays (read *holy-days*) gets you props for being ambitious, industrious, and dedicated. Climbing the corporate ladder takes such precedence over enjoying the fruits of labor that taking time off can make you feel lazy and worried about your future. Leviticus turns all that around. Rather than treating *holy-days* as intrusions on our time, Leviticus views holidays as sacred time, sneak peeks of eternity.

OFF THE CLOCK

Sacred time is God time. As God's people, we need it. Though Christians no longer keep these particular Levitical feasts, vestiges of them show up all over the Christian holidays. The Lord's Day has superseded Sabbath, but aspects of Sabbath still apply. We (supposedly) stop work in order to enjoy its fruits. We worship. We take pleasure in each other. We eat. Likewise with Passover in Leviticus 23:5. For Jews, Passover and the Feast of Unleavened Bread together serve as sacred remembrance of their rescue from slavery to the Egyptians (unleavened bread because they had to hurry to get out of Egypt). Jesus made Passover his Last Supper, and then the church made the Last Supper the Lord's Supper. Jesus took the bread and wine of Passover and announced that these were now his body and blood, shed for our rescue from slavery to sin. Paul joyfully proclaimed to the Corinthians, "Christ, our Passover lamb, has been sacrificed. Let us therefore celebrate the festival" (1 Cor. 5:7–8 ESV). Regrettably, however, we mostly celebrate the *funeral,* treating the Lord's Supper more as a time to bewail our sinfulness than to be glad for our redemption. Not that bewailing our sin is a bad thing (see chapter 9), but if it's the only thing we do, then I think we miss the supper's main point.

Perhaps the ancient Israelites missed the point too. Thus, God made sure they got back on target by ordering the Feast of Firstfruits (Lev. 23:9–14). The seven-day Feast of Firstfruits commemorated the barley harvest, the first crop to rise from the ground. Paul described resurrection as a harvest rising from the ground and the risen Jesus as "the firstfruits of those who have fallen asleep" (1 Cor. 15:20). This connection between Firstfruits and the resurrection makes Easter the Christian Firstfruits, always a joyful celebration. Promised to rise from the ground ourselves, we give thanks to God by giving him the firstfruits of our earthly harvests. We tithe as a way of showing that we mean it when we say God comes first in our lives.

Fifty days after Firstfruits (seven Sabbaths plus one day—the eighth day being that biblical marker for eternity) came the wheat harvest and time to party again. The Feast of Weeks or Pentecost (meaning "fifty"—Lev. 23:15–22) meant a feast of *leavened* bread, since nobody was in a hurry to get out of Egypt anymore. Jesus compared the kingdom of God to yeast—a little bit permeates an entire batch of dough and causes it to rise (Matt. 13:33). In the book of Acts, the Feast of Weeks was the occasion of the Holy Spirit's leavening that small band of believers into a huge force that through persecution and apparent defeat (just like the cross), overwhelmed the Roman Empire and took the gospel to the whole world. Pentecost remains the birthday party of the church.

During the Pentecost harvest, Leviticus reminds everybody to leave some of the crops for the poor to gather. This practice, called *gleaning* you'll remember, allowed the unemployed to enjoy the dignity of work, but it also allowed the unemployed to join the party. Kim considered her twenty-first-century gleanings to be "purchasing rations from local grocers, farmers, and the like," enabling them to enjoy the fruits of their labor rather than the sour grapes of always having to compete with "the military agricultural complex" for their profits. In our "tail-chasing economy that many suburban centers find themselves in," good gleaning means supporting "the local merchant as opposed to letting my money be funneled to a gazillionaire."

After Pentecost came the Feast of Trumpets (Lev. 23:23–25). Time to blow a horn. Trumpets sounded the start of the seventh month (a Sabbath month), the end of harvest, and therefore the biggest festival month on the Levitical calendar. The apostle Paul and the book of Revelation both blow trumpets to signal the end of harvest, though theirs is a harvest of metaphorical wheat. For Paul, the trumpet signaled the harvest of the righteous (1 Cor. 15:52; 1 Thess. 4:16); in Revelation, trumpets announced doom for the damned (chapters 8 and 9). Jesus alludes to both in his trumpet talk (Matt. 13:25–30; 24:31) about separating wheat (the righteous) from the weeds (the damned). The trumpet of the Feast of Trumpets is first and foremost a call to repentance (even in Revelation, the doomed aren't damned yet). Ten days after the horns (Lev. 23:26–32) comes the Day of Atonement (time to load the goat—see chapter 9 again). For Christians, you might think of Palm Sunday as Trumpets to Good Friday's Day of Atonement (though they are not ten days apart).

The Feast of Booths or Tabernacles (23:33) doesn't have as clear a Christian parallel. The Feast of Tabernacles features the pitching of temporary tents or "booths" that call to mind Israel's thirsty desert sojourn on their way to the Promised Land and how God himself traveled alongside in a mobile home of his own (recall Mary Frances's construction of her own tabernacle in chapter 3). The earthly Promised Land was but a foretaste of heaven itself. It was at the Feast of Tabernacles where Jesus declared himself to be the light of the world (John 8:12) and the water of life (John 7:37–38). Walter sees Jesus quenching the eschatological (end times) thirst that this feast signified.

I remember stumbling upon an observant Jewish neighbor of mine who had pitched her tent in the middle of a parking lot, fully abandoning the comfort of her urban condo in good Tabernacles fashion. Later, I met a gentleman in the suburbs who had erected a tabernacle on his back deck, only his opened up through his sliding glass door into his posh living room. I couldn't help but feel that he was cheapening the intent of the exercise. I also couldn't help but mention this out loud in his presence—in a joking way, of course. Knowing that I was a Christian, he came back at me with four simple words: "Plastic. Blinking. Nativity. Scenes." (He had a good point.)

Of course the *main* point of Tabernacles—at least from a New Testament perspective—was not to remember the Israelites' time in the desert (especially since they didn't spend *forty years* wandering around as a reward for good conduct). The main point of Tabernacles was to remind us how, as sojourners, we are still on our way to the real Promised Land (the new heaven and new earth—Rev. 21). In time God will usher his people into a new heaven and a new earth where he will abide with them forever. On second thought, perhaps that tent on the deck *did* prove more apropos, inasmuch as it was connected to something better. Tabernacles envisions that day when all of our temporary, shabby shelters will be shed for posh quarters, a day when redeemed creation will thrive in sync with God's time.

The command to keep these feasts is God's command to remember how this world is not our final home, that we are citizens of heaven and aliens on earth (but not in the UFO sense). All this should make you happy. If it doesn't, Leviticus says you are to be "cut off from [your] people" (23:29). The Lord does not tolerate party poopers.

A LEVITICAL LORD'S SUPPER

For our church's Communion service during the Levitical month, it made sense to celebrate the Lord's Supper in good Levitical, celebratory fashion. That we were gathered on a Sunday together and nobody was working (but me) covered the Sabbath requirement. Passover and the Feast of Unleavened Bread were taken care of by the wine (the Paschal Lamb) and the bread (matzo) of Communion, though we also had to have a leavened loaf to cover Pentecost. We couldn't get Mary Frances's tabernacle transported and set up, so we settled for lighting four candles to represent the lights lit at the Feast of Tabernacles. The first-century Tabernacles' light liturgy used four huge candlesticks, on top of which sat massive bowls of lamp oil with wicks made from the discarded trousers of priests—don't ask me why. We decided to just go with regular candles.

For representing Firstfruits, I couldn't get a sheaf of wheat, so I settled for a book about wheat with a pretty sheaf on its cover, which I was able to wave as a firstfruits wave offering (Lev. 23:15—though I looked like a firstfruitcake doing the wave). And then, just in case anybody felt they had shortchanged God earlier during the offering by not giving him their firstfruits, we put the offering plates back out with the following caveat: in compliance with the Feast of Weeks, the plates would be left unattended so that any who *needed* money could take rather than give (another effort at gleaning). This did two things. First, it helped people who needed immediate financial assistance (one homeless guy who stumbled into the service praised the Lord for hitting the jackpot, though he was very respectful and thankful in taking what he took). Second, it encouraged giving above and beyond what was normal because people liked the idea of helping people who needed money right then.

As for representing the Day of Atonement, that was easily covered by our confession of sin. And in keeping with Trumpets, since the trumpet is a call to repentance, we had someone blow a horn to get us started. Actually, we went authentic by having a guy bring in a shofar—a ram's horn he hadn't blown since Hebrew school as a kid. (He repented for blowing it so badly.)

All of the feasts, while rolling out the carpet for new creation, also set the table for the earthly feast of all feasts, the yearlong Feast of Jubilee (Lev. 25:10–55). Given that Jubilee was so huge, I couldn't cover it in a single Communion service. Since it was the epitome of all other feasts, I decided to devote Easter Sunday to it (with apologies to Firstfruits). Any preacher will tell you that the hardest sermons to preach are at Easter. It's not that the resurrection itself is hard to preach; it's that everybody already knows how the story turns out. You'd think if people were going to skip church, Easter would be the Sunday to do it. Nobody wakes up that morning thinking, *I wonder if they'll find Jesus in the tomb this year.* Instead, even with the story now in its two-thousandth season of reruns, people pack churches on Easter more than on any other Sunday.

Of course, it may be that people figure a predictable sermon beats a bad sermon. At least if you go to church on Easter you know what you're going to get. But not if you attended my church during the Levitical month. There were no resurrection reruns this time. Instead, I invited the crowd so sit back and enjoy an

Easter sermon from the book of Leviticus (well, maybe *enjoy* was overstating it a bit). The congregation started to squirm noticeably, but nobody walked out. Not even after I gave an overview replete with animal sacrifices and skin diseases (I could tell one middle school boy was psyched by all the gore!). I then mentioned how for serious believers, taking Leviticus seriously is not optional. Inasmuch as the whole Bible is considered to be the Word of God, we don't get to pick which parts to obey and which to disregard (at least, we're not supposed to). While skipping some parts of Leviticus may make sense, skipping chapter 25 makes no sense at all. Chapter 25 commands the remarkable (and even outrageous) practice of Jubilee.

LET'S START OVER

Every fifty years, a trumpet was supposed to blow (the word translated "jubilee"—*yobe*—means "blow the horn") to announce a wholesale overhaul of economic and social conditions. Jubilee signaled a new beginning, a time when all who had failed at life and work were given a do-over and when all who had benefited from others' failures let go of their gains. Land reverted to its original owners, debts were forgiven, slaves set free, and scores set back to zero. As a yearlong extension of the Sabbath, everyone took a year off to enjoy, stress-free, the fruits of their labor with thanksgiving. Of course in a predominantly agrarian society, the question undoubtedly arose as to how you would eat if you didn't work your land for a year. God took care of that. He declared, "I will send you such a blessing in the sixth year that the land will yield enough for three years" (Lev. 25:21). Even the earth needed a break. Jubilee represented Old Testament environmentalism at its best.

It represented Old Testament economic justice at its best too.

Jubilee prevented the amassing of wealth into the hands of a privileged few. Every fifty years, accounts were squared and equality was reestablished. Jubilee curtailed the human desire to accumulate more and more by yanking down social and corporate ladders. Greed got checked. The rich were kept humble and the poor were made hopeful. Everybody understood that we are tenants on this earth, not owners. All things ultimately belong to the Lord. People were not allowed to take advantage of each other in life or business, because to do so was to take advantage of God. Moreover, they were motivated to treat the poor justly since in the next go-round, once everything began afresh, those who were successful before might find themselves on the short end of the shofar.

This Levitical vision proves so captivating that a movement is currently afoot called Jubilee USA. Its purpose, supported by many churches, is to promote House Resolution 2634, titled the Jubilee Act for Responsible Lending and Expanded Debt Cancellation. (It was passed by the U.S. House of Representatives on April 16, 2008, by a vote of 285 to 132. The Senate is not yet living Levitically. The Jubilee Act—House Resolution 4405—was reintroduced on December 16, 2009.) In the world's most impoverished nations, the majority of the population does not have access to clean water, adequate housing, or basic health care. These countries are paying debt service to wealthy nations and institutions at the expense of providing basic services to their citizens. The United Nations Development Program estimates that thirty thousand children die each day due to preventable diseases. Debt service payments take resources that impoverished countries could use to cure preventable diseases. The Jubilee Act mandates debt cancellation for these countries. Ironically, these debtor nations have already paid back their debts time and again; it's the interest that's killing them. Once interest rates rose and compounded, repayment became impossible.[1] This explains why the Hebrew word for *interest* is from a root that means "to bite" (Lev. 25:36; *nāshak* means both "to bite" and "to lend for interest").

It may be that you've felt bitten of late. As I write this, the United States is mired in one of the worst recessions in history. While the causes of the recession are numerous, part of the blame is directed at the deregulatory demons released by Congress that allowed Wall Street to act like Las Vegas. Main Street banks passed on subprime mortgages to Wall Street investment banks, where they were sliced and diced and resold, all on credit. The word *credit* derives from the Latin *crederi,* which means "to believe." And everybody believed. While few people understand how Wall Street investment giants made all their money, there's no doubt that they made it. Billions of dollars in bonuses were paid out as naive homebuyers took out 100 percent mortgages on overpriced houses. Treating credit as assets doomed taxpayers to inevitable loss. Real estate in America had always been a good bet (or at least the good dream), so people figured the sky was the limit. But even the sky has its limits. The inevitable nationwide default on ever-riskier housing loans made a dead end out of both Wall Street and Main Street. The government was forced to intervene with huge infusions of cash to prevent the economy from seizing up—cash for which the government itself has gone further into debt to pay.

The crises of Leviticus 25 read like the subprime mortgage mess. A farmer fails at farming, defaults on a loan, and loses his land but not his obligation to his creditors. It reminds me of a time I stumbled onto the credit card bills of a family member I had agreed to help through school. I thought she was counting her pennies and being a good steward of my generosity, but it turned out that she had run up extensive credit card debt. Because I had chosen to financially expose myself for her sake, I ended up with the bill, which meant refinancing my house to pay it—that is, going into debt to pay debt. Had I been living Leviticus back then, chapter 25 would have allowed me to enslave this family member until she worked off the debt (v. 40). This may sound like sweet revenge, only Leviticus prohibits any harsh treatment of a person indebted to you (v. 39). I would have had to restructure payments according to her ability, and if the year of Jubilee arrived before she fully paid me back, her entire debt would be forgiven. Which sounds unfair until you realize that the bank that held my mortgage would forgive my debt too.

WISHFUL THINKING

Granted, all of this sounds completely unrealistic. So unrealistic that there is no evidence that Jubilee was ever observed. Though commanded by God, it never happened. Maybe it was deemed too impractical. Or maybe it just took too much faith to pull off. Or maybe those who'd made it to the top were too unwilling to let loose of their achievements and possessions. For whatever reason, Israel's unwillingness to follow the law led to their downfall. Redeemed from their slavery in Egypt, delivered into the rich Promised Land, God's people took advantage of his goodness. So much so that they lost their land and their freedom. If you've read the story, you know that the Babylonians ransacked Israel and drove its population into captivity. But that wasn't the end of the story.

Because God has a thing for sinners, he announced through the prophet Isaiah another shot at Jubilee. Speaking of the Messiah to come, Isaiah said,

> The Spirit of the Sovereign LORD is on me,
>   because the LORD has anointed me

to preach good news to the poor.
He has sent me to bind up the brokenhearted,
to proclaim freedom for the captives
and release from darkness for the prisoners,
to proclaim *the year of the LORD's favor*
and the day of vengeance of our God,
to comfort all who mourn,
and provide for those who grieve in Zion—
to bestow on them a crown of beauty
instead of ashes,
the oil of gladness
instead of mourning,
and a garment of praise
instead of a spirit of despair. (61:1–3, emphasis added)

But again, if you've read the whole story, then you know that this second shot at Jubilee went unfulfilled too. True, by God's grace, the Israelites were rescued from their Babylonian captivity; but human nature being what it is, their bad behavior quickly returned and the people found themselves in captivity again, this time to the Romans, with no hope on the horizon. But again, God has his thing for sinners. So he sent Jesus, who walked into his local synagogue, dusted off the book of Isaiah, and read those Jubilee promises again: "The Spirit of the Lord is on *me*, because he has anointed *me* to preach good news to the poor. He has sent *me* to proclaim freedom for the prisoners and recovery of sight for the blind, to release the oppressed, to proclaim the year of the Lord's favor" (Luke 4:18–19, emphasis added). The congregation might have appreciated Jesus' attempts to restore their hope had he not gone on and audaciously added, "Today this scripture is fulfilled in your hearing" (v. 21). It was as hard then as it would be now to envision your

Messiah as a homeless, unemployed carpenter from the bad side of town. So offended was the congregation by what sounded to them like a mockery of their plight that, the Bible says, "they got up, drove him out of the town, and took him to the brow of the hill on which the town was built, in order to throw him down the cliff" (v. 29).

Jesus slipped away for the time being, but in time, he'd get strung up as a criminal and a blasphemer. However, the New Testament imports an image from Leviticus to show what really happened on the cross. As you read regarding the Day of Atonement, once a year the Jewish high priest would take a scapegoat and symbolically transfer all the sins of the people onto it and then chase this scapegoat out of town to die, sometimes by tossing it off a cliff—just as the congregation in Luke 4 tried to do with Jesus. Jesus is our scapegoat. As the apostle Paul writes, "God made him who had no sin to be sin for us" (2 Cor. 5:21).

Everyone knows how the story turns out. Jesus rises from the dead. In doing so he establishes justice and yanks down the social and corporate ladders. He squares our accounts with God. He settles our debts. The poor are exalted and the weak lifted up. The last are first and the lost are found. Death becomes the way to victory. Sinners get a do-over. A new start. "[Jesus] died for all," Paul writes, "that those who live should no longer live for themselves but for him who died for them and was raised again....If anyone is in Christ, he is a new creation; the old has gone, the new has come!" (2 Cor. 5:15, 17). And not just for this life. Paul adds elsewhere, "We will not all die, but we will all be changed, in a moment, in the twinkling of an eye, at the last trumpet. For the trumpet will sound, and the dead will be raised imperishable, and we will be changed" (1 Cor. 15:51–52 NRSV). "Sound the loud trumpet," Leviticus sings. "Proclaim liberty throughout the land to all its inhabitants. It shall be a jubilee for you" (25:9–10 ESV).

A SOUR NOTE

Yet, like the Israelites, our tribe of temporary Levites struggled to experience the jubilation of Jubilee. No doubt part of that had to do with the lack of cooperation from banks and creditors. None were willing to set aside any of our debts (even for the month). Part of our struggle probably had to do with the ease with which so many of us reverted back to the way we'd lived previously once the month was over. Beards were shaved. Bacon was fried. Work was done on the Sabbath.

But still, something had changed within us. Andrew discovered one of Leviticus's beautiful ironies—namely, that only by taking on the burden of obedience can you find true freedom. For him, the Jubilee command to return property to its rightful owner meant deleting all the music he had downloaded through the music-sharing service Napster. He couldn't return all this music he'd "borrowed," but he could acknowledge that it was no longer his. When he'd first downloaded it (record companies would say he stole it), Andrew rationalized by reminding himself how rich those record companies were and that on the Internet, everything should be free. But heeding Leviticus, he realized that rationalization and holiness rarely mix well. So he dumped the music (and he had a lot of music), only to find himself enjoying the music he then purchased on the other side so much more. In Andrew's own words, "I was jubilated!"

We need the joy (and the freedom) Jubilee brings. All month long we'd been recording our adventures on video and then posting them on Facebook. How would we record Jubilee? We decided to make a final movie, but rather than something in documentary form, we decided to go with the genre of music video. The idea was that even if we couldn't fully pull off a Jubilee Year, at least we could produce a few jubilant minutes. And we decided to make it in time for the Easter service since Jubilee, appropriately, was our Easter theme. We wanted to show it in church and spread a little jubilation.

We pulled out a version of the folk tune "Ain't No Grave Gonna Hold My Body Down" (by the band Crooked Still). There's a line in the song about "God's people dressed in white," so we dressed in white (which has Easter significance, if not Levitical significance). We then walked over to the graveyard beside the church and commenced to dance on the tombstones, symbolic of the good news of resurrection, the ultimate Jubilee. People watching us make this video were convinced we were crazy (if not disrespectful! Though if Easter is about anything, it's about disrespecting death). But c'mon, we'd been living by Leviticus for a month! Our celebration was not that the month was over. We were actually a little sad about that. Our celebration was about discovering that obedience could indeed be a joy—a discovery we hoped would not end with the experiment itself.

HEAVE-HO HO HO!

Among the reasons that obedience is so rarely joyful is our tendency to equate obedience with burdensomeness. Jesus tries to lighten the load by referring to his yoke as easy and light (Matt. 11:30—a yoke is a wooden bar or frame by which two draft animals, typically oxen, are joined at the heads or necks in order to pull a heavy load together). While Jesus may be saying that the load we now carry is light because there is no load (you know, since Jesus came to fulfill the law), I argue that the load of law still applies, only now Jesus helps us haul it. If anything, Jesus' command that we take up a cross to follow him (Mark 8:34) is heavier than the law itself. Isn't there supposed to be joy in that (1 Pet. 4:16)?

While such joy may be strange to imagine, it's unforgettable once experienced. If ever you've taken seriously your commitment to Jesus—be it by loving enemies, refusing to chase after money, telling the truth, confronting injustice, serving the poor, or forgiving debtors—then you know whatever hardship you encounter only serves to make you stronger. Call me crazy (the people in the graveyard did), but chances are good that if you've ever put yourself out there for the sake of Christ and the gospel, then you've experienced a power, a spiritual juice, a joy of obedience that energizes you to put yourself out there even further.

For Lisa, her obedience was tied to love—both love for Jesus and love for her father, who suffered from Alzheimer's. Leviticus 19:3, reiterating the fifth commandment, says, "Each of you must respect his mother and father....I am the LORD your God." For Lisa, respect entailed honor, reverence, and esteem. She wrote,

> I have been struggling with how to maintain this attitude in the details of caring for a parent who is deeply afflicted with Alzheimer's. Each moment of interaction brings countless thin lines between respect and disrespect. How do you maintain the intent of this commandment to honor your parent at the end of his life? In making sure he takes food in his mouth when he won't open it, in listening to him when he makes no sense, in maintaining him when he can't keep himself clean, in obeying unspoken and unformed requests? This commandment is a struggle for children and adolescents and becomes quite a different struggle again as we care for our parents in their later life. In my youth I was running from this calling, laughing as I turned my back. I now find myself running to it with full desire to fulfill God's calling. I pray I do.

Finally, as the month was wrapping up, I got a phone call

from a gentleman in our congregation who had been reading the posts and watching the videos. He wondered if Leviticus would apply to his particular dilemma. He had delayed the sale of a house he owned in another state for more than two years so that he wouldn't have to evict two tenants, both professing Christians. Nevertheless, the tenants put off paying this owner, offering one excuse after another, month after month, until they'd run up a back rent of more than twenty-five thousand dollars. The owner, still willing to help, refinanced his mortgage in order to lessen their financial burden. Eventually, however, unable to sustain two mortgages on his own, he ended up having to sell the house and evict the tenants anyway. He called me because now he wasn't sure what to do about the back rent. It was causing him a truckload of stress. Feeling righteous myself (obedience can do that too), my knee-jerk response was to suggest he seek legal assistance and get what was rightfully owed him. It wouldn't have been an unbiblical route, especially given that it was a last resort.

However, since I was in the midst of thinking about Jubilee when he called, I couldn't help but ask (albeit hesitantly) whether he'd considered just forgiving the debt. I hesitated because I knew most people would consider forgiving such an enormous debt as irresponsible (how were those tenants to learn their lesson?), unfair (what about the owner's rights?) and frankly, nuts. Yet at the suggestion I sensed a freedom and an immediate lightness in the owner's voice. He sheepishly asked, "Would that be okay?" He too knew that to forgive such an enormous debt was irresponsible, unfair, and yes, nuts—which, of course, was precisely what made it feel so much like Jubilee, so much like grace. And grace, I assured him, is always okay.

Chapter Eleven

Laying Down the Law

Follow my decrees and be careful to obey my laws, and you will live safely in the land. Then the land will yield its fruit, and you will eat your fill and live there in safety.
     —Leviticus 25:18–19

One of the best aspects of the public nature of our Levitical experiment was the feedback it generated from readers and observers (via Facebook, blogs, or other Internet mentions). A lot of this feedback came in the form of questions, some less serious than others. For instance, one perceptive and sarcastic set of questions (available on many religious skeptics' websites) found its way to our Facebook group. It sought some "interpretive assistance" with a few specific Levitical laws (which I provided). It went something like the following:

> Burning a goat or bull as a burnt offering (Lev. 1) creates quite the literal stink. The Lord likes it (Lev. 1:9), but my neighbors hate it. Should I take out my neighbors? [No, only God is allowed to smite your neighbors. You must love your neighbors—Lev. 19:18.]

Leviticus 25:44 states, "Your male and female slaves are to come from the nations around you; from them you may buy slaves." As an American, does this mean that I can only purchase slaves from Mexico and Canada? [Actually, this only applies to neighboring nations of *Israel*. So neither Mexicans *nor* Canadians would apply. You would have to purchase an Egyptian.]

What about people who say that eating lobster (Lev. 11:10) is just as abominable as being gay (Lev. 18:22) since they're both in the Bible? [I'd have to go with Jesus here. He declared all foods clean (Mark 7:19), which definitely removes the abominableness. Jesus isn't on record about homosexuality explicitly, but given his attitudes toward nonmarital sex in general, I'm guessing you'd best settle for eating lobster.]

Leviticus 21:19 prohibits anybody with a broken foot from coming near God in the tabernacle. There's also something about bad eyesight. How bad does my eyesight have to be? Can I have a sprained foot that's not broken? Would that preclude me from offering sacrifices to God? [It probably depends on whether you have "an itching disease or scabs" too—Lev. 21:20.]

I know lots of guys who cut the hair at the sides of their heads or clip off the edges of their beards as Leviticus 19:27 forbids. What should be their curse? [Extreme embarrassment due to male-pattern baldness.]

Leviticus 11:7–8 says that pigs are unclean and that "you must not eat their meat or touch their carcasses; they are unclean for you." Does this include playing football? [Luckily, footballs haven't been made from actual pigskin for decades. Footballs are now made of leather—hide from an animal that chews its cud and is cloven at the hoof (Lev. 11:7). Nevertheless, you probably shouldn't play football on weekends inasmuch as some might construe that as working on the Sabbath.]

A certain relative who goes to church with me has a garden where he's planted two different kinds of seed. Worse, he wore a blended-fiber sweatshirt while he did it. Leviticus 19:19 expressly prohibits both. When I informed him of his transgressions, he let loose a string of expletives in direct violation of Leviticus 24:15. Do we have to gather the "entire congregation" together to put him to death (Lev. 24:16) or can a few of us burn him with fire as Leviticus 20:14 allows whenever a man has sex with both a woman and her mother? [Unfortunately, burning the man who sleeps with both his wife and her mother was also public. So yes, you'll need to gather the entire neighborhood. You will also need to hear a direct, audible command from God—Lev. 24:13.]

Sarcasm aside, these sorts of questions did get to the core of the Levitical dilemma. How do you apply the law to real life? We believers can be excellent compartmentalists—adeptly managing to cordon off our "real lives" from our "spiritual lives." The sense is that faith is either irrelevant to most of what we do or makes us feel awkward outside of Sundays. But if Leviticus does anything, it breaks down this compartmentalization by infusing faith into everything—our food, our clothes, our bodies, our relationships, our work, and our play. Leviticus illustrates what it looks like to love the Lord with all of your heart, mind, soul, and strength (Deut. 6:5), which Jesus labeled the greatest commandment (Mark 12:30).

Mary Frances changed her sheets during the Levitical month (which she does religiously anyway: "I may not keep kosher, but I'm all about cleanliness!"). Yet rather than a routine household chore, it became a powerful lesson in God's grace. As she pulled the dirty sheets from her bed, she noticed the pattern to be a red print on white. Given all that she'd read in Leviticus, her thoughts immediately went to blood, sin, and uncleanness—all Levitical no-nos. She then noticed how the clean sheets she had laid out happened to be "white as snow" (Isa. 1:18). She wrote that she couldn't help but be reminded of how Jesus stripped us of the "unclean coverings that we insist on hiding under. He washed us of our sin, and he made us clean. Who knew that sheets could be holy?"

Granted, thinking theologically about changing your sheets isn't everyone's idea of integrating faith and life. Not to mention rethinking your menus, keeping watch over your skin, keeping track of your sins, or checking the labels on your clothes. Plenty of readers who logged in to our Levitical adventure thought our experiment to be a waste of time. One reader went so far as to label the whole experiment foolish. If keeping Leviticus does nothing to save you, then how can disobeying Leviticus do anything to condemn you? Another reader concurred. He called our project just another evangelical entertainment trick.

Then there were those who took issue with our approach. One reader criticized our attempt at living Levitically by noting that whatever we did it wasn't living according to the book. To live by Leviticus is not to capriciously decide what parts to follow and how to follow it. Leviticus is an all-or-nothing proposition, the reader said. Rather than a potluck, Leviticus is a family dinner with strict parents who demand that you clear your plate or go hungry. Were blasphemers stoned? Were menstruating women quarantined? Were animals sacrificed? Were infected people sent out of town? If not, then we weren't really living Leviticus.

We all struggled with the all-or-nothing nature of Levitical adherence. Fortunately, another reader, in response to our critics, cut us some slack. She wrote that if you actually read Leviticus cover to cover, there's no way you could expect anybody to do everything it says. That would be crazy. Crazy enough that we did what we did, she thought. Still, our goal was not to figure out shortcuts. We wanted to be obedient, yet we also realized how as Christians, an interpretive filter was in order. For instance, given that Jesus died for our sins, making animal sacrifices for sin would have been the epitome of *disobedience*. Some of our critics extrapolated this instance to the whole of the law. The old Jesus-obeyed-the-law-so-we-don't-have-to thing again. They quoted Paul's letter to the Galatians, "All who rely on observing the law are under a curse, for it is written: 'Cursed is everyone who does not continue to do everything written in the Book of the Law.' Clearly no one is justified before God by the law, because, 'The righteous will live by faith'" (Gal. 3:10–11).

Another Facebook post said our month would have been better spent memorizing Galatians than toying with Torah. Didn't we understand that the law is over now that grace has come? Why did we think that the apostles never required Gentiles to keep Jewish law? It was a straitjacket! An anchor that weighed people down! The only thing it's good for now is to make us glad we have Jesus so that we don't have to worry about it anymore.

Being a lover of wordplay, I once tried to come up with a term for what many read as Paul's contention that believers in Jesus who have died to the law are therefore freed from the law. What would you call a kind of Christianity for which there were no rules or regulations? Since the Greek word for law is *nomo*, how about *no mo nomo*? Or maybe just a simple *bye-law*, or perhaps *illegalism*. Of course all this terminology presumes Paul actually advocated a lawless Christianity—which he didn't.

A LAW-ABIDING CITIZEN

The law, as God's prescribed standard of righteousness and holiness, condemned disobedience. Paul went so far as to sound as if he were blaming the law for his disobedience (though he adamantly denies this). He wrote to the Romans, "Once I was alive apart from law; but when the commandment came, sin sprang to life and I died [spiritually speaking]. I found that the very commandment that was intended to bring life actually brought death" (Rom. 7:9–10). How does this happen? If the law is not sin, how exactly does sin's badness feed off the law's goodness to cause sin? In two ways I think.

First, we all know that one fairly reliable way of getting somebody to do something we want them to do is to say, "Thou shalt not…" Growing up in the 1970s, I had long hair, and my dad hated it. He was always on me to cut my hair. (I used to wear it shoulder length, parted in the middle, feathered back. I was a stud.) When it came time to get my driver's license, my dad said I could only drive if I got a haircut. So I played the religious card: Jesus had long hair. To which my dad said: Jesus did a lot of walking too. Naturally part of the real reason I grew my hair so long was because it made Dad so crazy. Had he told me how much he loved my locks, chances are I'd have been at the barber that afternoon. There is a sinister power in reverse psychology, a power Paul described as sin turning the law into taboo. The more the law condemned Paul's covetousness, the more Paul coveted (Rom. 7:8).

At the same time, however, the law that entices insubordination in some also induces *overboardination* in others (how's that for a word?). As a type-A Pharisee, Paul knew about this sort of sin too, the sin of trying to attain righteousness through good behavior. Ironically, throughout the Gospels, Jesus condemned such attempts at self-righteous compliance as worse sins than blatant defiance. Why was this? Because the law, for all of its goodness, was never designed as a means to achieve righteousness. Righteousness was always meant to come by grace and never by merit. Again, the ancient Israelites were already chosen people before God laid down the law. God didn't choose Israel to be his people because he knew they could be law-abiding citizens. God chose them because he loved them. The law's purpose was never to save anybody. Its purpose was to show saved people how to live a saved life.

Most of the Pharisees understood this at first. They didn't start out as the pompous, self-righteous legalists we vilify them as. Most of the Pharisees began as sincere, humble, God-fearing men who simply wanted to live holy lives and maybe even play golf on weekends (though never on the Sabbath—swinging a club would have been too much like work). For them, living holy lives meant devoting themselves to safeguards and incentives to obedience, not so different from well-meaning Christians who construct detailed accountability checklists designed to promote piety—checklists that ask not only "Did you spend sufficient time praying this week?" but also "Did you *lie* about how much time you spent praying this week?" The problem with such checklists is not so much that a failure to comply causes guilt and shame, but that *successful* compliance inspires pride, warping people previously humbled by grace into people who don't need grace anymore. The same sin that perverted the law into *taboo* perverted it into an achievable list *to-do*.

This brings me back to our critics. Given the law's ability to elicit both guilt and pride, the best thing to do actually might be to stop worrying about obedience to the law because Jesus has done all the work. But we know that's not right, because then we would miss out on all the joy! Besides, Jesus would have never reiterated a Levitical command like "Love your neighbor" or preached the Sermon on the Mount if he'd already taken care of everything himself. Obedience to the law is good; it's just not *sufficient*. It will never make you righteous or holy. Only grace can do that. Whether by shortcoming or overdoing, the prodigal and proud and everyone in between all fall short of God's glory (Rom. 3:23), which means that attaining God's glory can only come as God's gift. God's law as righteous standard impeaches human sin, but only in order to impose human reliance on God's grace that we may reliantly live in accordance with those same righteous standards. It is by grace we are saved. It is by grace we obey.

After the experiment was over, our tribe of Levites-for-a-month generally agreed that obedience was no longer capitulating to a set of rules, but rather a pathway to relationship whereby the goodness, holiness, awesomeness, and joy of God came clear. To a person, coming face-to-face with the demands of holiness exposed our sinful tendencies and stretched our faith (and our need for grace). Holiness as day-to-day reality tore down the dividing walls we'd erected between faith and real life. Food and clothing were understood to be as important to God as personal relationships and personal ethics—just as they are to us. God cares about how we treat one another, but he also cares about what we wear and eat—so much so that Jesus tells us not to worry about it ourselves (Matt. 6:25–26).

Brandy considered making herself a WWLD bracelet, akin to the old WWJD bracelets—"What Would Jesus Do?"—only replacing "Jesus" with "Leviticus" since we assume what Jesus did was obey Leviticus. (Ironically, people used to poke fun of those old WWJD bracelets by sarcastically asking what Jesus would wear and eat.) Brandy wrote, "This experiment kept me more mindful of what the Lord asks of me than I ever typically am on a daily basis. I don't usually stop to ask if what I am doing is honoring God, except when it comes to a 'big decision' of some sort—and half the time, not even then. I really started to appreciate the constant reminder of the presence of the Lord in my life and the way that presence changes my life in very tangible ways."

Ian concurred. "What I've learned is that a study of the Old

Testament law—either in part or in whole—may seem like a waste of time when you're in the fairly common modern-Christian mind-set that all that stuff's been done away with and 'all you need is Jesus,' but it has a very real and tangible value in that (for a limited time, at least) it can help you to live deliberately, with greater vigilance, keeping God more frequently in mind, and more easily remembering the concept of holiness within your day on a moment-to-moment basis."

"Ideally," Brandy added, "my sense of God's presence and the sense of tangible change will be something that carries over well after the last day of the Levitical month."

PASS THE PORK

Once the month was over, Brandy's first video post from her office cubicle had her happily munching down on a spiced hot dog. Paul did the same, filming himself savoring a slice of bacon the first morning after. Ian was even more ardent, writing about starting off the day after "with a nice breakfast of bacon, continue it with a bacon-based lunch, and perhaps complement the evening with some manner of bacon-themed dinner. You probably think I'm kidding."

Thomas almost blew his effort at keeping kosher by eating pork *on* the last day of the Levitical month. He was at a deli counter on the last day when the butcher passed him a piece of ham to taste. Which he did, to his subsequent horror. "A whole month of difficulty and discipline in depriving myself of pig products and I'd failed with only a couple of hours to go," he moaned. "What a waste of time and taste buds. Disappointment and anger and bitterness toward the fool who sliced the sin and handed it to me. But then, lying in bed at 2:30 a.m., I remembered! I had started my month of Levitical Living in Northern Ireland, five hours ahead of the rest of the tribe! So my month ended not at midnight EST, but at midnight GMT! Joy! GMT is five hours ahead, so I could have eaten a pig stuffed with shrimp cooked on the Sabbath by an adulterous periodic woman with an infectious skin disease in a polyester shirt at 7 p.m. and had nary a worry. Off to sleep having lived Levitically for two hours more than the mandated month."

Despite all of our best intentions, each of us speedily regressed back to our default, pre-Leviticus posture. We laid down the law. Whether the category was food, clothing, relationships, or ethics, Levitical living was not a sustainable lifestyle. Neither, for that matter, is living by the rest of the Bible. Thomas wrote, "That I fail to be perfect in adherence to Old Testament laws for holiness and right living is not so different than my failing to live purely and lovingly in my New Testament reality. I still set the standard high and make the effort authentic, but failure is allowed for and should not be made more of than it merits. Nor is guilt anymore necessary after the Levitical sacrifice than after the Jesus forgiveness. Feeling guilty after either is a waste of emotion more usefully invested elsewhere."

In the spirit of investing her feelings of guilt elsewhere, Kristi (the opera singer) decided that her lack of success at keeping the law after the month was over (not that she would have described her Levitical month as "successful") could at least be turned into music. Inspired by the Levitical month, she composed a cantata titled "Obedience." "I wanted it to be a conversation between me and God," she wrote. "His message never changes, despite my somewhat arrogant and naive proclamation of my intent to obey completely, or my falling into temptation that leads to sin." Kristi cast God as a bass/baritone ("No way is God a tenor!"), the deep resonant voice suffice to demand that his people live righteous and holy lives. Like the Israelites of old, Kristi cast herself as one eager to follow God and do all that the law commands ("Riiight"). Kristi wrote, "One problem that I identified during the Leviticus month was my tendency to see God's salvation as a magic wand—a wand that will somehow fix everything all at once, enabling me to live a life of holiness, without my having to learn obedience, as even Jesus did!" (Heb. 5:8).

In her mind, the magic wand approach was without "both nuance and direction. I've thought of holiness in general terms, whereas God was very specific with the commandments that he gives. Of course, such specificity only magnifies our shortcomings. This is where learning about the sacrificial system came in," Kristi wrote. "Knowing that the sacrifices didn't atone for intentional sin was essential for my understanding the importance of Jesus' death. And this is why I bookended the cantata with Psalm 51:17 ["The sacrifices of God are a broken spirit; a broken and contrite heart, O God, you will not despise"]. I try to obey. I can't. So Jesus obeys for me. Hence the title, "Obedience." However, Jesus' obedience doesn't let me off the hook. Instead, it puts me back *on* the hook. So, even though I am unable to obey to secure my salvation, Jesus' death and resurrection enable me to walk straighter and straighter. And when I can't, I can cry 'Have mercy on me!' And he does."

It was a beautiful cantata. Kristi recruited a string quintet and a fine God-sounding baritone for the performance. The congregation loved it (even the ones who weren't opera fans). They also loved the video we put together summarizing the things we learned from the month. We showed it in church too. In it, Kim echoed Kristi's sentiment regarding Jesus' obedience on her behalf. She said, "I have an overwhelming need for grace. Overwhelming. This month put my sins in front of me, close to me, all over me, and I felt them being washed." "Holiness is hard," Thomas concurred, "but obedience and adherence alone help not a jot. Prayer within a living and loving—and therefore obedient—relationship with him who came to fulfill the law is, however, another story."

LEVITICAL LESSONS LEARNED

This was the real story: the Levitical month ended up not being about our ability to obey enough, but about our ability to trust God enough to live the life he's determined to be the best life to live. Brandy wrote, "How do I live a life set apart to God so that it shows every day? Now that I am eating shellfish and not wearing oil and ash, what about my life must show that God has called me to him for a purpose? Now that the month is over, I think I feel relieved; disappointed in myself; a little sad; and wondering what happens next. What about my *life*—not only my external appearance—will be pointing my friends and family and colleagues to the Lord? Somehow, I think that is the question I'm meant to be asking, in the aftermath of this Levitical journey."

Inasmuch as living a holy life is living a *peculiar* life, the expectation was that people would notice. For the heavily bearded Paul, this wasn't necessarily a good thing. "I've learned that it stinks to be set apart," he reiterated on the final video. "I didn't like it. As a white man in America, I'm comfortable that everybody is pretty much like me where I work. Nobody else has a beard. Somebody called me Ted Bundy! Not that I've been conforming all my life, but this month I've really felt out of my element." However, one man's discomfort was another's opportunity. Thomas mentioned how tough it was for him "to explain all of this to people who were not Christians or who don't believe in God. Before the experiment I thought it was difficult enough to satisfy them intellectually with what I believed and why, but explaining something like this Leviticus month made me look even more freakish or unusual. I find it frustrating and I feel inadequate to explain, but once I pushed through that, I found myself having deeper conversations about faith this month than I have ever had before."

For Brandy, Facebook provided an unexpected conversation. "This is a shout-out to my first—and only—Facebook friend to ask me what was up with this whole Leviticus thing. I really appreciated it! I wondered all month what my other friends who were not in this experiment thought about it. I wondered if anyone had been reading, if anyone was interested, if anyone was a little weirded out, or mostly if folks just ignored it as just another news feed item out of the scores Facebook dumps on me every day. We had a cool conversation. We talked about what the experiment had been like, and the experience of doing it with other people, and how it was making me really, really think when I read the Bible. I guess, in a way, this has been part of me trying to be much more open about my faith—and about what really goes on inside me in general—with people I meet outside of my Christian circle."

Facebook also produced some expected pushback. Not long after our "Living Leviticus" Group appeared, a contrary Facebook group formed called "Leviticus Was On Crack." The group affirms the Bible as a collection of well-respected documents that form a guide to living a happy and moral life . . . except for Leviticus!

WON'T YOU STAY MY NEIGHBOR?

While the idea of the Levitical month essentially did begin as a gimmick and an easy way to load up on sermon illustrations, no serious encounter with the Bible ever fails to affect you. I continue to wrestle with the nature of obedience, even though I think I understand (and have experienced) its challenges and joys. To be honest, my biggest problem is that most days I don't want to obey. Loving God and my neighbor leaves too little love for *me*.

Maybe this is another reason that Leviticus (as well as the Christian life itself) must be done with God and each other together. I'm convinced that one of the reasons that each of us so easily slipped back into our default modes of obedience is because we stopped being a tribe. We no longer shared dinner together, we stopped posting on Facebook, we stopped checking in on each other and forgot to keep praying for each other too. Without the Levitical glue, we basically went back to our solitary, private lives (me and Jesus). As many writers, theologians, and pastors have noted, the biggest threat to Christianity in America is not secularism or materialism (or even Satan) as much as it is individualism. To be a Christian is to be a *member* of the body of Christ (Rom. 12:5). The extent to which we try to do it on our own (or even just me and Jesus) is the extent to which we will always miss the mark.

Not wanting to let go quite so easily, Mary Frances left up the tabernacle she had constructed inside her tiny apartment for an extra two months after the experiment was over. This surprised her friends, one of whom asked whether it was strange to walk into her house and see it every day. Mary Frances wrote that it wasn't strange at all. What *was* strange was that she no longer noticed it.

> Like a bad piece of art or a roommate's ugly lamp, this crazy tabernacle that I had constructed to be a daily reminder of God dwelling *with* me—something I couldn't ignore if I tried since it took up a good 25 percent of my apartment—had become just like another piece of furniture, part of the backdrop of my life.
>
> After I first constructed the tabernacle, it was like being hit in the face with God's presence every time I walked into the house. But after three months of living with this thing in

my apartment, I can't remember the last time that happened (for all of you Levitical naysayers out there, I *know* that my ramshackle "tabernacle" was not the actual dwelling place of God—it was just a visual aid, people!). Like so many other things in life, my attention got diverted elsewhere and the novelty wore off. However, today as I sit on my couch, I am very much aware of its absence. As a New Testament Christian, I know that God's Spirit is with me today just as much as yesterday, but it does feel like something is missing now. It's hard to believe that I could forget to notice something like a tabernacle sitting in the middle of my apartment, but even harder to believe that I actually forget to notice God. But I do. Every day. All through Leviticus we read about offering God our firstfruits. Yet from me God mostly only gets my last fruits, if that.

Leviticus reminded me (and by "remind" I mean "slapped across the face") of the power and holiness and justice and, yes naysayers, of the grace of God. He holds us to a high standard, not because he wants us to suffer, but because he wants us to *live*. Leviticus shows us that we were created and chosen for a higher calling. That we are the "haves," not the "have-nots." That although we often bring nothing but our last fruits, we worship a God who has given us the gift of himself in Jesus. "I will put my dwelling place among you....I will walk among you and be your God, and you will be my people" (Lev. 26:11–12). You may think I'm crazy, but I'm going to say it anyway: I love Leviticus. Amen and amen.

FINALFRUITS

As a minister, I loved being alongside others as we wrestled with this peculiar book to which we have staked our lives. Thinking back to the story of Jacob wrestling with God (Gen. 32:24–30), I'm reminded that *Israel* means "to wrestle with God." Inasmuch as Israel's story is our story, perhaps wrestling with God is part of what it means to be faithful. There is a tendency to preach the gospel solely as the solution to life's problems—rather than to fully disclose how the gospel also introduces a brand-new set of problems. I've yet to hear a recent believer describe coming to Jesus only to have his or her life get worse. Okay, maybe not *worse*, but definitely *harder*.

Hard is not bad. For the Christian, hard is necessary. Difficulty exposes our weaknesses and our feeble faith, but these are good things as far as Jesus is concerned. Human weakness has always been his preferred means of doing things. As he said to the apostle Paul, "My grace is sufficient for you, for my power is made perfect in weakness" (2 Cor. 12:9). The same with weak faith. It's never the *amount* of faith that matters as much as the *direction* in which it is pointed. Even weak faith is strong as long as it is pointed at Jesus. The law helps us here. As Galatians explains, "The law was put in charge to lead us to Christ" (3:24). Insofar as Leviticus exposes our weaknesses, it shows us Jesus' strength. Or again as Galatians puts it, "For through the law I died to the law, so that I might live to God....It is no longer I who live, but Christ who lives in me" (2:19–20 ESV). Do you see me loving my neighbor and loving my enemy? Do you see me caring for the poor and the stranger? Do you see me striving for holiness in every aspect of my life? Do you see me being thankful and prayerful and joyful? Do you see me sharing my possessions and not storing up for myself? Do you see me forgiving those who've hurt me? Do you see me totally devoted to God? Do you see me holy as God is holy? That's not me. "I no longer live." It must be Jesus in me.

By his grace we are saved. By his grace we obey. It's the only way to be perfect.

Bibliography

Balentine, Samuel E. *Leviticus*. Louisville: John Knox Press, 2002.

Bauer, Walter (author), and Frederick William Danker (editor). *A Greek-English Lexicon of the New Testament and Other Early Christian Literature*, 3rd ed. Chicago: University of Chicago Press, 2001.

Harrell, Daniel. "The 30-Day Levitical Challenge." *Christianity Today*, August 2008.

Harris, R. Laird, Gleason L. Archer Jr., Bruce K. Waltke. *Theological Wordbook of the Old Testament* (Two Volumes). Chicago: Moody Press, 1980.

Hartley, John E. *Leviticus*. Waco, Texas: Word, 1992.

Milgrom, Jacob. *Leviticus: A Book of Ritual and Ethics*. Minneapolis: Fortress Press, 2004.

Ross, Allen P. *Holiness to the Lord*. Grand Rapids: Baker Academic, 2002.

Telushkin, Joseph. *Jewish Literacy*. New York: HarperCollins, 2001.

Wenham, Gordon. *The Book of Leviticus*. Grand Rapids: Eerdmans, 1979.

Notes

CHAPTER TWO: A VIRTUAL TRIBE OF LEVITES

1. "The number of American households that play computer or video games has risen to 68 percent, a three percent increase over 2008, according to the Entertainment Software Association, a group that represents U.S. computer and video game publishers," http://www.theesa.com.

CHAPTER FOUR: BAD SKIN AS SIN

1. See http://www.southerngospel.com/Family/Singles/1167828/page-2/ (accessed 21 February 2010).

CHAPTER FIVE: DOES GETTING WORKED UP ABOUT THE SABBATH COUNT AS WORK?

1. An adapted version of this story appears in my book *Nature's Witness: How Evolution Can Inspire Faith* (Nashville: Abingdon, 2008), 103.

Chapter Six: Loving Your Neighbor with an Unshaven Face

1. Thomas Merton, *The Sign of Jonas* (New York: Houghton Mifflin Harcourt. 2002), 242.

Chapter Nine: Loading the Goat

1. Hannah Gruber, "Living Out Leviticus," *Heart and Mind* 22:2, Spring 2009, 2.
2. Walter reminded our group that *propitiation* is the English word that emphasizes the appeasement of God's wrath. Some would argue that the better translation is *expiation* (RSV), which focuses not on wrath to be appeased but wrong to be expunged. There's an ongoing theological debate over which word is better.
3. See http://www.boston.com/news/local/massachusetts/articles/2010/03/10/a_rite_thats_passing.
4. Adapted from The Book of Common Prayer (New York: Church Hymnal Corporation, 1979).
5. Bard Thompson, *Liturgies of the Western Church* (Philadelphia: Fortress, 1961), 197; Book of Common Prayer, 331.
6. Miroslav Volf, *Free of Charge: Giving and Forgiving in a Culture Stripped of Grace* (Grand Rapids: Zondervan, 2005).
7. Martin Luther, *Three Treatises*. From the American edition of *Luther's Works* (Philadelphia: Fortress Press, 1978), 304; Harold J. Grimm, ed., *Luther's Works*, vol. 21 (Philadelphia: Fortress Press, 1957), 150.

Chapter Ten: Let Us Keep the Feasts

1. See http://www.jubileeusa.org.

About the Author

Daniel Harrell is senior minister of Colonial Church, Edina, Minnesota. For twenty-three years he served as a minister at Park Street Church in Boston. He is also the author of *Nature's Witness: How Evolution Can Inspire Faith* (Abingdon, 2008), as well as numerous articles that have appeared in *Leadership Journal, Christianity Today*, the *Christian Century*, and *Regeneration Quarterly*. He holds a PhD in developmental psychology from Boston College, and has lectured at Fuller Seminary, Gordon-Conwell Theological Seminary, Gordon College, and Boston University. He lives somewhat obediently by grace in Minneapolis with his wife and daughter.